TOTAL

QUALITY

MINISTRY

TOTAL

QUALITY

MINISTRY

Dr. Walther P. Kallestad

Steven L. Schey

Augsburg
MINNEAPOLIS

TOTAL QUALITY MINISTRY

Cover design: Hedstrom/Blessing, Inc.
Inside design: Evans McCormick Creative

Library of Congress Cataloging-in-Publication Data

Kallestad, Walther P., 1948–
    Total quality ministry / Walther P. Kallestad, Steven L. Schey.
        p.   cm.
    Includes bibliographical references.
    ISBN 0-8066-2778-6 (alk. paper)
    1. Pastoral theology.   2. Total quality management—Religious aspects—Christianity.   I. Schey,. Steven L., 1950– .   II. Title.
BV4011.K28   1994
253—dc20   94-25107
                                                                            CIP

The paper used in this publication meets the minimum requirements of American National Standard for Information Sciences—Permanence of Paper for Printed Library Materials, ANSI Z329.48-1984.   ∞™

Manufactured in the U.S.A.   AF 10-27786

98   97   96   95   94   1   2   3   4   5   6   7   8   9   10

We dedicate this book to Dick Gunderson,
president and chief executive officer
of Aid Association for Lutherans,
who ignited the idea of Total Quality Ministry
and is a world-class leader for Total Quality.
Thanks, Dick, for your friendship and partnership
in ministry.

Contents

Preface

Total Quality Management is a process for achieving high quality within an organization. It has its basis in the understanding that quality is measured by the customer and that quality means meeting or exceeding the customer's expectations 100 percent of the time. With this understanding of quality, the Total Quality Management processes employ organizational principles and resources in ways to meet this quality goal.

Total Quality Management has been discussed in the business world for many years. The leaders in the quality revolution include W. Edwards Deming, Philip Crosby, Joseph Juran, Tom Peters, Stephen Covey, and others. Over the last 15 years, the ideas and processes developed by these individuals have been refined into several key principles that are today known and taught as Total Quality Management.

This book develops the translation of those processes into the Christian church. Because these processes have come from the business world, the concepts and terms may not be readily understood by persons involved in congregational ministry who have had no previous contact with TQM. Therefore, it becomes necessary to define the business terms for application in the congregation.

The first term that needs definition is *customer*. The business community and all of us living in a consumer society understand the meaning of customer. Yet we may not have ever associated the term *customer* with the church. Because quality is always centered on the customer's expectations, it is essential also that congregations understand this term. How can this best be translated into what we understand as congregational ministry?

The business community understands its customer as one who pays or might potentially pay for the product or service offered. This implies some kind of transaction taking place, such as a fee for a service or product. Other terms for naming the customer could be patron, client, purchaser, user, and so forth. For the Christian congregation, the people who partake or might potentially partake in the services offered could be considered the customer. Another term that might provide better recognition among congregations is *constituent*. Webster's dictionary defines constituent as "an essential part." A constituency is defined to be "the people involved in or served by an organization." Both terms, customer and constituent, have relevance for congregations and will be used throughout this book.

The definition of *services* includes much more than that of the worship service. Services provided by congregations include education classes for all ages, small group meetings, counseling, facilities for community activities and elections, preschool and/or elementary school classes, nursery child care operations, and the list goes on. With this idea of service, and considering all who may partake or use the services, *congregations define the customer to be anyone who is in any way affected by its ministry.*

Traditionally, congregations may have thought of its customers as its members. The new definition of customer expands beyond that of members to include visitors, friends of members, neighbors of the church, community leaders, the media, other churches, other pastors, and the list goes on. The expanded list of persons affected by the congregation is what is understood by *customer* in this book.

The next term that needs definition is *quality*. In the for-profit community, quality is measured by the customer, and quality means meeting or exceeding the customer's expectations 100 percent of the time.

The same definition may be used for quality in ministry. It means meeting or exceeding the expectations or needs of the customer in such a way as to fully satisfy him or her, and to do it in a manner without deficiencies. You will discover in the pages of this book that the quality we strive for in the church goes beyond customer satisfaction to transformation. The processes of Total Quality Ministry lead to the development of the climate and environment in which transformation of lives can occur.

In this book, the processes of Total Quality Ministry are organized in this acrostic.

Q uick Responsiveness to Needs
U nity of Purpose
A nticipation and Expectation
L eadership Development
I nvestigating Results
T raining, Education, and Development
Y ield in Transformation of Lives

This acrostic is used as an aid in learning and remembering the seven principles of Total Quality Ministry. The seven principles are summarized here.

1. Quick Responsiveness to Needs—The focus placed on the *customer/ constituent:* identifying who she or he is, determining needs, and meeting those needs and expectations.
2. Unity of Purpose—The focus and direction of the organization in relationship to *God's purposes,* revealed in the congregation's mission and vision and the planning that results.
3. Anticipation and Expectation—The *planning processes* that by design will meet or exceed the expectations of the customer and will provide feedback for *continuous improvement.*
4. Leadership Development—The importance of the commitment and drive of *leadership* of the congregation in implementing the Total Quality Ministry processes.
5. Investigating Results—*Statistical thinking* that seeks to measure by valid and accurate means the important parameters of a process, for use in the decision-making process.
6. Training, Education, and Development—The importance of the *staff and volunteers* in the overall quality process. The importance of gaining employee/volunteer involvement in the process so that each sees his or her role in the overall quality of ministry.
7. Yield in Transformation of Lives—The "bottom line" for your ministry. *Life transformation* is the work of the Holy Spirit, and Christian congregations are called to be involved by Jesus' command to, "Go therefore and make disciples of all nations, baptizing them in the name of the Father and of the Son and of the Holy Spirit, and teaching them to obey everything that I have commanded you" (Matthew 28:19-20a).

While the above order of the principles fits the "QUALITY" acrostic, it does not imply a level or order of priority or importance. Rather, each principle is important as it adds to the whole. It is the view of the authors that the final principle does indeed carry the greatest importance as it is understood to be the reason for congregational existence.

With the terms *customer, services,* and *quality* defined, the balance of business terms and concepts will be defined as they are discussed in the book.

Lest the reader misunderstand at this point, this book is not about the continuous improvement of lives, as though we could by some might of our own make ourselves more acceptable to God. The processes of Total Quality Ministry consider the continuous improvement in the way congregations do their ministry. This excellence and quality in ministry leads to repeat customers and creates a climate and environment for the work of the Holy Spirit in the lives of people.

Introduction

Quality was a standard of measurement when God created the earth and everything on it. Everything God made was 100 percent free from defects. Ninety-nine point nine percent was not good enough.

Today, if 99.9 percent was good enough:

- 22,000 checks would be deducted from the wrong bank account in the next hour;
- 1,314 phone calls would be misplaced in the next minute;
- 12 newborn babies would be sent home with the wrong parents;
- 2 large passenger planes would crash at an international airport every day;
- 20,000 prescription medications would be incorrectly written this year;
- 18,322 pieces of mail would be mishandled in the next 60 seconds;
- 315 entries in Webster's Third New International Dictionary would be misspelled.

Quality can never be compromised in any area of life, especially ministry. In the parable, Jesus left 99 percent of the flock of sheep to find the 1 percent that was lost. Jesus died on a cross so that everyone, not 99 percent, but *everyone*, might be saved. The quality of God's love is 100 percent, 100 percent of the time.

Good Enough Isn't Good Enough

An inner city church in downtown Philadelphia decided that its community was too comfortable with second best. When it came to building a community room, they decided that they would not build second best, not when safety and security were concerned. This room was built first rate. It was built with excellence, not leftovers. It was to be a signal to the people not to settle for second rate. The church said that good enough was no longer good enough!

Several years ago, corporate America received a rude awakening to the foreign competition intrusion into its market share. For decades, good enough was good enough for many U.S. companies. The companies believed that Americans would continue to come to them to receive their products and services. Suddenly quality became more important to the consumer than loyalty to U.S. companies. More and more companies are now awakening to the need for quality improvements.

Total Quality Management ranks among the greatest tools in use today for increasing the quality of products and services in the corporate world. Implementing the principles of Total Quality Management pays great dividends in customer satisfaction, employee satisfaction, product and service design and quality; and it ultimately shows up as a positive influence on the bottom line. One of the thrusts in Total Quality Management is zero defects. Good enough is no longer good enough.

Total Quality Ministry takes the principles of Total Quality Management and interprets them for use by the Christian church. Total Quality Ministry does not try to make people with zero defects, nor does it try to make people the product of continuous improvement. It does seek continuous improvement and zero defects in the way ministry is accomplished. Through the implementation of Total Quality Ministry, Christian congregations can achieve many of the same benefits achieved by the corporate world, including effectiveness at the bottom line, even though the bottom line for congregations is significantly different from that of the corporate world.

The purpose of this book is not to make a business process out of ministry but to make the business of ministry a quality process.

Implementation of the processes of Total Quality Ministry will produce many benefits.

1. TQM addresses conflicts and power struggles in the church by shifting the focus from accumulating power to giving power away. Empowerment of people is a key in building great churches, churches with a great sense of God's ministry.
2. TQM generates higher morale by more carefully evaluating the process instead of criticizing the person.

3. TQM helps manage time, talents, and treasures—thus providing more discretionary time, greater excellence in ministry, and a stronger financial foundation to build up effective ministry.
4. TQM emphasizes God's mission and vision for the congregation, which leads to unity in the body. Congregations turn attention from the urgent (but often unimportant) to the important matters.
5. TQM creates a deeper appreciation for the persons with whom ministry is carried out. Keeping the focus on the customer and her or his needs helps prevent congregations from becoming inward in focus.
6. TQM provides a climate where deficiencies and problems are prevented. Greater energy may then be focused on the ministry rather than fighting fires and correcting problems.
7. TQM ultimately provides the atmosphere for persons who do not know Jesus Christ to be open and available to hear the good news and to be receptive to the work of the Holy Spirit.

Building a Total Quality Ministry depends on laying a total quality foundation:

> According to the grace of God given to me, like a skilled master builder I laid a foundation, and someone else is building on it. Each builder must choose with care how to build on it. For no one can lay any foundation other than the one that has been laid; that foundation is Jesus Christ. Now if anyone builds on the foundation with gold, silver, precious stones, wood, hay, straw—the work of each builder will become visible, for the Day will disclose it, because it will be revealed with fire, and the fire will test what sort of work each has done. If what has been built on the foundation survives, the builder will receive a reward.
>
> 1 Corinthians 3:10-14

The foundation for Total Quality Ministry is Jesus Christ. He is the rock upon which every great ministry is built. TQM presents a process that will help everyone who is serious about quality ministry build upon the foundation already laid, Jesus Christ.

The authors have been actively pursuing and implementing the processes of Total Quality Ministry for many years, without realizing the parallels from the for-profit philosophy of Total Quality Management. Recent events have led to this understanding, and in research for this book, it has been discovered that many other congregations are implementing many of these principles and processes as well. Some congregations have already conducted their own interpretation and are experiencing new growth and vitality. But there are many congregations who are searching for ideas and tools to become more effective, efficient, and focused in ministry. The principles of Total Quality Ministry can provide these ideas and tools.

Dr. Walt Kallestad has been the senior pastor at Community Church of Joy in Glendale, Arizona, for over 16 years. He has led this congregation to become one of the fastest growing Lutheran churches in America. Since 1978, the congregation has grown from a membership of about 200 people to nearly 7,000 today, with several thousand more calling Community Church of Joy their church home. While still a small congregation, Walt recognized that he could not carry out the mission and vision for Community Church of Joy on his own. He promised God that the credit for any success would always go to Jesus Christ. With God's help and direction, and Walt's leadership, the success of Community Church of Joy in terms of growth and life transformation is largely due to consistent efforts in implementing many of these principles of Total Quality Ministry.

Steve Schey is senior administrator at Community Church of Joy. He was called from management in the corporate world to full-time church administration in 1989. He spent six years on the board of directors for the church prior to joining the staff. Having actual experience in the process of quality improvement, he understands the terms and processes used in Total Quality Management and is able to translate them into the successful implementation of Total Quality Ministry.

This book is the collaborative effort of Walt and Steve to present a summary of a transformational process through which church decline may be reversed, with its success being measured in reclaimed lives for Jesus Christ.

To understand more about the commitment to total quality, the authors cite the following example. During the 1980's, Steve was an engineer in a large engineering and manufacturing company in the Northeast. For many years this company had been a leading supplier of a particular product, but the market for this product suddenly disappeared. Because management believed the market would reappear within five to ten years, the focus of the company shifted to completion of backlog orders, customer service, and product enhancement. Nevertheless, the company believed it was still just waiting for the market to reappear.

With the reduction in market, several internal changes occurred, including the layoff of many employees. While company management struggled with a new purpose, it also became aware of a philosophy of improvements in quality through "culture change," which could lead to many bottom-line enhancements. A company's culture is its formal and informal way of accomplishing its work. By changing the culture, employees become more committed to the company, each other, and to the products produced. In the process, morale is enhanced and productivity increases with less sick time and greater employee satisfaction. As employees gain greater work satisfaction, they work better together and work becomes a collaborative effort. The company costs are reduced, and it becomes more competitive with greater net income.

As a middle manager, Steve was involved in many of these steps. The company spent millions of dollars on consultants and internal costs to attempt this culture change, but after a year, nothing more was heard of this process. The culture change process failed at that company for at least three basic reasons.

1. LEADERSHIP

The engineering company executives implemented the culture change process as a means of improving the bottom line but were not committed to making the necessary changes that were identified in the culture change process. Also the leaders' personal morals and ethics can positively or negatively impact crucial cultural transitions.

2. VISION

The company did not have a vision for the future. The employees did not know why the company was in business. They could not answer questions about the company's future as a supplier in the existing market or as a service company.

3. EMPLOYEE COMMITMENT AND EMPOWERMENT

The employees did not feel the commitment of management, did not trust them to ensure job security through the process, and were restricted by internal controls from easily performing their work functions. Frustration led to a further lack of commitment and a cynical attitude toward the success of the effort.

Today many organizations are looking to Total Quality Management to improve their performance and bottom line. The three areas noted above, which were failures for that engineering company, are crucial to the successful implementation of Total Quality Ministry.

Many congregations today parallel the difficulties of that engineering and manufacturing company. Many churches have not yet understood that the paradigm for churches has changed. Under the old paradigm, children were educated in the mainline denomination and grew up loyal to that denomination. In a Christian society, a church simply needed to exist and be loyal to its traditions and it would grow as people came to its doors.

The "market" for churches is no longer the same as it once was. Wishing for the market to return will not change the facts nor will it reverse decline. Just as that engineering company failed to face facts, many congregations continue to deny their circumstances. It will take leadership, vision, and commitment in congregations to bring about a real change.

This book is not intended to be a complete guide toward implementing a Total Quality Ministry process in congregations. While there are examples included, it is not intended to be all-inclusive. In addition, many of the examples come from the experience of the authors at Community Church of Joy. This is not intended to imply that these examples are to be copied. It is the conviction of the authors that each congregation is uniquely called by God and in its unique setting will determine the best approaches for implementing the principles of Total Quality Ministry. The principles remain the same, but the implementation may differ. Several examples of the implementation of the principles in other congregations are cited.

The implementation of Total Quality Ministry is also not a function of the size of the congregation. While Community Church of Joy has been blessed by God in its growth, there are congregations of much smaller size that are also successfully implementing quality principles.

This book is intended to be a wake-up call and to present ideas to churches on what is possible. It does provide the basis for an implementation strategy and training program for congregations interested and motivated toward quality improvement.

The implementation strategy is being developed at Community Church of Joy at this writing. By the time of publication of this book, that strategy will be well developed. In March of 1994, Community Church of Joy began the journey to full implementation of Total Quality Ministry through this developing strategy. In addition, a pilot program for implementation of Total Quality Ministry in a variety of settings was begun. More will be said of this in later chapters.

In Galatians 1:24, Paul writes, "And they glorified God because of me." While Total Quality Ministry can improve a congregation's ministries, the goal is not to point to the congregations who are revealing God, but to point to God who is revealed in that congregation so that people will glorify God because of that ministry!

Chapter 1
A Quality Story

Total Quality Ministry Stays Ahead of Tomorrow

October 19, 1993 would be either the end or the new beginning of the dream. We believed that God was faithful. We believed that God had led us to this point. We had worked for years on the relocation of Community Church of Joy. We had worked through the questions, doubts, contingencies, sidetracks, and resistance to find the land, but we still needed one more thing—the money! The owners of the land were not going to wait with land prices rising fast and property being developed. *This was our deadline!* If we failed, the land contract would be lost. The investment committee was meeting to determine whether they would provide the financing. One thing was certain; it would take a miracle!

The story starts much earlier than 1993, however. As far back as 1978 we dreamed of a ministry that ministered to the whole person—spiritually, physically, emotionally, and mentally. Such a ministry needed room to grow. Walt dreamed of a 200-acre campus that contained not only the church facilities, but also preschool, elementary, and secondary education facilities; a Bible school or college; a retirement center; health and fitness centers; recreation facilities; restaurants; a performing arts center; and a leadership training center. It would be a place where people want to dream, to walk, to worship, to serve, to play, and to learn. It would capture the enthusiasm and joy of the Christian life, where people care about and for one another. This would be a place where people invited their friends, relatives, neighbors, and co-workers to grow along with them.

Steve was elected to the congregation council in 1984 and served as chair of the Future Planning Committee. As a nuclear engineer and mathematician, Steve knew about projections, statistics, and how to solve problems, but he didn't know how to dream. When Walt suggested we would have to move, he couldn't believe it. The sanctuary had just been completed, and we still had eight acres of undeveloped land. Why move?

Dreams Fuel Vision

Membership continued to grow, and in 1986, Steve projected this growth into the future. If growth continued at its current rate, we would have to move by the end of 1994.

By 1988, membership had grown to 3,500 baptized members. With the increase in attendance, it became clear the projections were quite accurate. The congregation council began to evaluate the options available to us in light of what was seen as a clear Holy Spirit inspired vision of the future of Community Church of Joy. We could not simply wait for overcrowded conditions to stop people from coming. The vision gained momentum. The council's analysis concluded that the path to which we were being called was to relocate.

This gave greater focus to the congregational strategic planning that was also in progress at this time. Input to that planning from everyone involved confirmed the fact that the new facility must be developed. Consequently, the 10-Year Strategic Plan was adopted by the congregation, although no one yet knew where the property would be.

Vision Becomes Reality through Planning

The existing 14-acre campus was not completed. Some could not understand why we were looking to relocate when half the existing property was still a vacant, dirt lot. We did need to make another major building decision at this time to better serve our existing needs. Our children had run out of classroom space on Sunday mornings, and our staff spilled out of the original space into several portable offices. We needed to build in order to keep serving people's needs and fulfill our mission. The size of the new building was determined to be that which would best allow us to maximize the parking space, the sanctuary space, and the education space. Growth projections indicated that all of these three would be at maximum utilization within 6 months of each other in 1994. We needed to build this building and complete new parking in order to survive another four years until 1994.

The Family Life Center was built in 1990 while we began the search for the right piece of property for relocation. Investigation and negotiation started with several locations. One site was chosen to prepare the conceptual master plan, but the negotiations were complicated by bankruptcy and foreclosure. In the spring of 1992, we knew we were running out of time. If we were not ready to move within a few years, we would strangle ourselves with overcrowding and start to decline.

Plans Require Action

The congregation became acutely aware of the situation and enthusiastically supported the resolution to purchase 200 acres and to relocate as soon as possible. We still did not have a site under contract.

In late 1992, the land that was of greatest interest to us was purchased from bankruptcy, and we began negotiations in earnest. We had no money. How do you negotiate without finances? Nevertheless, we were confident that this was the right site. It was currently a citrus grove located directly off a freeway interchange; it had no neighbors as yet, but was located in the fastest growing community of metropolitan Phoenix. It had tremendous visibility with nearly one-quarter mile of freeway frontage. Developers were buying up land in the area, and houses were being built at an amazing rate. Did we stand a chance against them in the negotiations?

Responsible Action Starts with Prayer

Several key friends of Community Church of Joy met with the leadership of Joy on the property and prayed. We prayed that this property would be a place where thousands of persons would come to hear about the love of Jesus and would develop a relationship with him as Friend, Savior, and Lord. We prayed for guidance with the financial responsibility. We prayed for the land owners. We prayed for God's will to be done through Community Church of Joy at this site.

Prayer Works

The owner of the land refused to see us until we were very close to the price he wanted. He finally agreed to have lunch with Walt. Through prayer, his heart was changed. He said he knew that he should not split up the 658 acres he had for sale, but for some reason he was excited about our project. He agreed to negotiate in earnest. He started coming to our worship services and is now a regular attender.

The 200 acres we wanted were expensive. The sacrifice required would be substantial. We signed the purchase contract in January 1993. We had until May to come up with over $3,000,000 to close escrow. Through the generous support of the congregation and friends of Community Church of Joy, we were able to generate a substantial amount of cash, but not enough to complete the purchase. We traveled all over the country to talk with others about this project. Everyone was excited, but most said, "Talk to me when you own the land."

Work Like It All Depends on You, But Pray Like It All Depends on God

Community Church of Joy is not a financially wealthy church. As with most churches that reach out to nonchurched people, finances are always tight. We have discovered that it takes four to seven years before a nonchurched person will give generously. Money is often the last area of one's lifestyle that is surrendered to God. In those first years with the church, the person needs the ministry and is often contributing financially well below the average long-time member. We had existing debt on the recently completed building and the sanctuary, so it was even more difficult to obtain new financing. We had equity, but ultimately a church is only worth what someone else is willing to pay for it.

We had tried local banks, large out-of-state banks, foundations, and unconventional sources. Now our loan request was being considered by Aid Association for Lutherans (AAL). Walt and Steve had first met with AAL in the Wisconsin office earlier in the year. Now we were on our way to Appleton, Wisconsin, to inform AAL about the ministry that was happening at Joy. Our plane to Chicago was delayed, and although we ran from one terminal to the other, we watched as our connecting flight departed the runway. Calling the AAL office, we explained our situation. Although the president had a very tight schedule, he agreed to meet with us when we arrived. Upon our arrival at AAL, we found that not only had the president stayed after normal hours, but several of his senior staff stayed as well. We spent several hours together, whereas, if our original flight had arrived on time, we only would have had an hour meeting. We gave thanks to God for turning this delay into a blessing.

God's Delays Are Not Necessarily God's Denials

AAL had been considering our request for a loan, but the size of the loan was a problem. Our lack of financial reserve and existing debt caused AAL to lean toward denial. After extensive phone conversations, the AAL vice president agreed to fly to Phoenix to see the property. He immediately recognized the great potential and the exceptional worth of the property itself. He agreed to recommend approval of the loan.

On October 19, 1993, AAL approved the loan. We closed escrow on the land in January 1994, and we are on track toward building the campus of our vision! The dream that started 15 years ago is beginning to take shape in physical form!

The results of the first ten years of Walt's service as senior pastor at Community Church of Joy closely matched the strategic plan he wrote in 1978. We believe that the blueprint developed for Joy in 1978 helped drive the decisions and short-term goals that resulted in ultimately reaching our long-term goals. The new strategic plan through the year 2000 is also directing our decisions and short-term plans. We believe that in ten years we will achieve what has been planned!

Follow Dreams through Vision to Plans into Reality, through Prayer!

God delights in quality plans and continual prayers. Our focus over the past fifteen years has not been to develop a monument to Joy but to pro-vide a ministry for people. We have provided a place where people can enthusiastically invite their friends and family. Joy was built to be a place where hurts could be expressed and needs met. It was to be a place where people would get to know Jesus better. It was to be a place where church and business leaders would be taught Christian morals, ethics, and values. It was to be a place where people cared for each other. It was to be a place where the love of Jesus and the grace of God so overwhelmed people that their lives would be forever changed.

This is a story about Community Church of Joy. But it is also an illus-tration of the principles of Total Quality Ministry. Those principles as they relate to ministry at Joy are what follows.

1. *Quick Responsiveness to Needs.* The whole purpose of the relocation of the church is to meet the needs of people—our customers. It seeks to provide what they need and even that which they may not know they need—the life-transforming love of Christ.
2. *Unity of Purpose.* The search for land was driven by our mission and our vision. God was sending people to us. We needed to provide the physical structures to meet their needs.
3. *Anticipation and Expectation.* The dream of providing many new ministries in a new location was developed through quality planning and expert outside consultation.
4. *Leadership.* This vision was so internalized by the leadership that we believed we were on the property and solving future problems before the contract was signed. The leadership of Community Church of Joy so led and informed the congregation that 88 percent strongly supported the resolution at the congregational meeting.
5. *Investigating Results.* This plan had its basis in the collection and analysis of measurable data. We were not guessing. Facility planning and timetables had a statistical basis.
6. *Training, Education, and Development.* This plan so involved the employees that many had made specific building design criteria requests before financing the land was assured. The director of physical plant even prepared detailed drawings of his support facility on the property.
7. *Yield in Transformation of Lives.* Above all, this plan considered the final yield in transformed lives, and who can count the number of people who will be forever changed by the love of Christ on this property into the twenty-first century!

This book is about Total Quality Ministry. Community Church of Joy and many other churches are on a journey toward total quality. What many of these churches do every day follows closely the principles of total quality. You are invited to join together with us on this quality journey found in the following chapters—and beyond!

Chapter 2

Q uick Responsiveness to Needs
U
A
L
I
T
Y

Pastor Bob found first hand that churches having a governing system of committees and councils move very slowly, and they insist on resistant control instead of responsive empowerment. When Pastor Bob wanted to start a second service at St. Stephen's, he found the process for approval to be less than effective in quickly responding to people's needs.

Many of the people in the community were unchurched. Pastor Bob discovered that the most effective way to attract these people would be through an alternative worship service.

Bob's idea was introduced in September at the church council meeting. The council decided to study the issue more carefully. A four-month study was commissioned.

The findings were presented in January the following year. At that monthly meeting the concern was raised that going from one worship service to two would split the church. This concern was then directed to a task force to discuss in every member's home. Months later the whole idea was brought to a congregational vote where it was rejected by two votes.

There was nothing quick about the process, and there was nothing responsive to the people in the community. The process followed in this case was probably more disruptive and divisive to the congregation than a quick decision to proceed would have been in September. A decision to proceed would have been based on the needs of the customer and not the needs of the organization.

This story was paraphrased from the October 1993 issue of *Minnesota Monthly*. It was part of an article, "Impresario," by Laura Billings and is reprinted here by permission.

Bill Conner goes on a fact-finding mission while the rest of us sleep. Before 8:00 a.m. on Sundays, he packs his two small children into his silver Acura Vigor, coasting away from his Edina home and casing communities for likely converts. He takes note of the houses you live in, the cars you drive, the clothes you wear, the markets you shop. He learns things about the audience he cannot learn behind his desk at the music theater. If residents of the Minneapolis/St. Paul area are not coming to the Ordway as he thinks they should, he tours the neighborhood to find out why. "The suburb Eagan should do well for us and it never does, so I go out there about once a month. But we are finally beginning to understand Burnsville."

Conner seems to be gleaning important information during these early morning jaunts. Since he started three years ago, the theater has raised its subscriber base from 3,300 to 31,000. In three years, the Ordway has undertaken a radical paradigm shift, changing its mission from an opulent nonprofit venue from its four principle users into an aggressively entrepreneurial arts organization. There is a new market in the Twin Cities for touring shows as it has been raised from 17th to 6th largest musical theater market in the U.S.

Conner says that they must make their art relevant to Minnesotans of all colors and that they must move away from raising money and concentrate on earning it. "If you don't keep moving and changing, you're dead."[1]

Successful businesses in the world today are studying the audience— the customer. Instead of saying "this is what we do, like it or not," they are beginning to ask "what do you want?" The paradigm has changed. Successful churches and congregations can learn much from their customers and constituents.

DETERMINATION OF CUSTOMER/ CONSTITUENT NEEDS

In order to determine the customer/constituent needs, we must first focus on the question "Who is our customer/constituent?" J. M. Juran in

Juran on Quality by Design identifies two types of customers: external and internal. We will focus on the external customer here and the internal customer in Chapter 7.

The term *external customers* is used by Juran in the sense of persons or organizations who are not a part of the company but who are affected by the companies activities.[2] Using that definition in the church, we can substitute the word *congregation* for company. Our customers are those people that are in some way affected by what is done by the congregation.

Using this definition, we must expand our view of customers beyond that commonly held by most congregations as "our members" to all those touched by our ministries. A short time of reflection will expand that list to include first time visitors, friends of members, vendors or suppliers, staff, volunteers, community groups using our facilities, neighbors, media, community leaders, other churches, other pastors, and the list may go on. You may have precinct voting on your church property, or a support group such as Alcoholics Anonymous may meet there. You can add them and other similar groups to your list of customers.

Pastor Vern Anderson is the pastor of Peace Lutheran Church in New London, Minnesota, a city of 900 people. He is also trained in the principles of Total Quality Management through the Army Reserve. Using many of these principles, he began teaching and training his congregational leadership. The church council grew in confidence and competence. Looking again at his "customer," he began to see his whole area as a mission field. The whole community became potential customers. Through this new vision of customer and through the trained laity, he has increased his average worship attendance from 300 to 600.

Each of the customers you identify will have particular needs. Our responsibility in ministry may not be to meet all needs for all people, but we are responsible for knowing our customer's needs and meeting those to the best of our abilities. Each of us serves using the gifts that have been given. Total Quality Ministry seeks to make the most of those gifts.

Once the Customers Are Identified, We Can Discover What They Need

In our congregation, we determined by graphing worship attendance figures that the attendance at the 8:30 Sunday morning worship service had declined over a period of two months. We initiated a survey at that service to solicit a response on areas of satisfaction and dissatisfaction. The response led us to make a few changes in music selection and style. The result was that attendance was restored and continued to grow.

Methods of determining the needs of people may vary greatly. Some examples of ways to determine the needs are explained and illustrated below.

1. SURVEYS

Conduct formal or informal surveys of people. The survey of attenders at our 8:30 worship is one example. At Community Church of Joy we often conduct informal surveys of groups of people. We also have conducted statistically valid surveys by selecting sample sizes and using random calling methods or distributing written surveys. They are a great tool to not only identify the needs but to check your customer satisfaction with how you are meeting those needs. Following is an example of a telephone survey we conducted involving 10 percent of our membership selected in a random manner.

CONGREGATIONAL SURVEY
Telephone Survey—10 Percent of the Congregation

1. How did you first come to attend Community Church of Joy?

2. What is the one thing you like best about CCOJ?

3. What worship service do you attend?
    ____ Sat. ____ 8:30 ____ 9:30 ____ 10:30 ____ 11:30

4. Why do you prefer that service?

5. How often do you attend? ____ weekly ____ biweekly
    ____ once a month

6. Is there anything about the service you would like to see changed?

7. Do you regularly participate in any other programs or activities of the church?

8. If yes to #7, which do you attend?

9. If no to #7, what is keeping you from participating?

10. Is there anything involving these programs that could be improved to increase your enjoyment and involvement?

11. Do you have any children living at home?

12. If so, do your children regularly participate in any program or activity?

13. If yes, which programs? If no, is there anything we can do to make it easier for them to attend?

14. If you use the nursery, how would you rate it on a 1-10 scale?

15. What do your children enjoy most about the programs they attend?

16. Is there anything that could be done to make these programs more enjoyable?

17. On a 1-10 scale, how useful is the church newspaper to you?

18. As you may know, financial contributions are lower this year than projected. What do you think is the primary reason for the lower level of giving?

19. Is your family better off, about the same, or worse off economically than they were a year ago?

20. On a 1-10 scale, how is CCOJ fulfilling the needs of your family?

21. What should the church be doing, or what is lacking?

22. Have you invited friends, neighbors, or co-workers to church?

23. If yes to #22, on a 1-10 scale, what was their response to CCOJ?

24. Are there any other comments you would like to make concerning CCOJ?

25. How many people are in your household?

26. What is the age bracket of adults in your home?
____ 21-30 ____ 31-40 ____ 41-50 ____ 51-60 ____ over 60

27. What is the age bracket of children in your home?
____ 0-5 ____ 6-12 ____ 13-18 ____ over 18

We Need to Understand Before We Can Be Understood

2. LISTEN

Many people will tell you their needs if you will really listen to what they are saying and not saying. Through counseling opportunities you may determine needs within your customer base. For example, following a tragic event where a member's child was murdered while walking home from a movie theater, we discovered a need for a support group for Parents of Murdered Children. Many people will not give you direct feedback but may respond to a suggestion box or other anonymous ways of expressing their needs.

Be alert to verbal and nonverbal expressions while listening. Never overlook the details that you may think are trivial but actually may matter greatly to the customer. The customer's perception may seem wrong, but you must respond to that perception. It is reality to him or her.

3. MESSAGE EVALUATION

How are people responding to your Sunday morning messages or sermons? Are they asking questions that you are not answering? Are you answering questions they are not asking? Are your messages relevant to the concerns, attitudes, and difficulties of your culture? To help us check the relevance of our messages, we use a system of message evaluation along with an evaluation of the worship service. Evaluation forms are distributed to specific individuals, and they are also available for others who want to offer their evaluation. Following is a copy of the evaluation form.

MESSAGE RESEARCH AND EVALUATION TEAM
WORSHIP SERVICE EVALUATION FORM

Service Date: _____ Service Time: _____
Evaluate the service from the perspective of a guest who is unfamiliar with
the church or the gospel.
Music: Choruses (singability, leadership), choir groups, solo and instru-
mental presentations (quality, style of presentation).

Message: Content, use of stories, presentation style (facial expressions,
gestures), listenability, applicability, length.

Technical: Sound, lighting, staging, temperature of sanctuary.

Service Continuity: Consistency of theme, dead spots, ushering,
announcements, scripture, and prayer.

Overall Impression: What climate did you experience: welcomed?
accepted? ignored? excluded? enthusiastiac? calm? rushed? Use your
own words.

TAKE COMPLETED SURVEY TO PASTOR IMMEDIATELY
FOLLOWING SERVICE.

---

4. CULTURAL STUDIES

Demographic information is available for your community. There is
much information available about your customers/constituents from census
surveys, marketing studies conducted by big and small businesses, the
Chamber of Commerce, educational institutions, the denominational
offices, and other sources. Businesses conduct detailed business plans before
investing in an area, and most will share that information with you. You
will learn about cultural backgrounds, income levels, married and single
households, age profiles, home ownership, and much more that may be
useful in determining needs. This will aid in knowing and understanding
the people and what is happening to them in this time and culture. You
can then respond by helping them hear the gospel in their own context.
Community Church of Joy is very much a baby boomer congregation in a

community of baby boomers. We already know many of the needs of this generation from studying what has been written about them. We then use feedback from them to tell us whether or not we are on target in ministry with them.

5. RESPONSIVENESS TO NEGATIVE FEEDBACK

Frequently people will not tell you what they need but will gladly share with you what they don't need. Use negative feedback for positive results. We recently had several comments that the sound was too loud at a worship service. The people all liked the live musicians playing the trumpets, trombones, and saxophones, but they could not hear the vocals very well above the instruments. The problem was solved by installing plexiglass shields around the band to reduce the sound level of the instruments. Provide ways for people to inform you of their complaints and their suggestions, and act quickly on them. Your customers will appreciate this. We have placed wish list cards in the pew racks and collection boxes at the doors to get instant feedback from worshipers (see sample below). You may also want to consider conducting exit interviews with households and staff leaving your church. Whether or not their departure is a friendly one, provide time for their candid feedback on the ministry. Remember that a disgruntled customer only tells others about her or his pain, but a happy customer will share a more objective picture.

JOY'S WISH LIST

Name _____ (optional)   Date _____

Phone Number _____ (optional)

We at Community Church of Joy are very concerned about improving the quality of our ministry to effectively meet your needs. Joy's wish list simply asks for some of your creative ideas, whether they be a certain topic you would like addressed in the sermon or a special class focusing on a specific topic. Our main purpose is to better relate to your needs. So, if you would fill out this card and drop it in our wish list box, located at the three main exits of the sanctuary, we would appreciate it.

_____

_____

_____

_____

_____

_____

6. BE YOUR OWN CUSTOMER

Evaluate yourself from the viewpoint of your customers. Try to eliminate your knowledge of the ministry, and look at what you provide as if you were your own customer. Be an observant customer at another church or ministry event. Compare what you notice there to what a customer would see in your ministry.

7. DISCONTINUE A SERVICE

If we question the effectiveness of a particular service that we provide for our customers, we may discover our customers' needs by discontinuing that service to see who notices. Those who notice may express their feelings about the necessity for the service. If no one notices, it was probably a waste of time. Even if some customers notice the loss, there were reasons why its effectiveness was questioned. There may be work needed to improve it.

> To believe that whatever we do is a moral cause, and should be pursued whether there are results or not, is a perennial temptation for nonprofit executives—and even more for their boards. But even if the cause itself is a moral cause, the specific way it is pursued better have results. There are always so many more moral causes to be served than we have resources for that the nonprofit institution has a duty—toward its donors, toward its customers, and toward its own staff—to allocate its scarce resources for results rather than to squander them on being righteous.[3]

8. FOCUS GROUPS

Consider gathering interested parties in a group discussion on a particular topic. Have a plan for engaging everyone in the conversation. While you will gain valuable feedback, consider that a strong or vocal leader may tend to sway the group's focus or feelings.

9. COMMON NEEDS

There are other needs that people have for mental, emotional, physical, and spiritual health. Providing opportunities for sports activities, counseling, education and growth are common opportunities for ministry. Many of our customers do not know of their need for Jesus Christ, although we know their need. Meeting their spiritual need *is* our primary focus. Meeting the other needs allows us to keep our customers while the Holy Spirit works on transformation.

It is appropriate to focus on the needs of people as we consider our congregational purpose. As Christians, we seek to follow Christ and his example. He comes to us—his customer. He meets us where we are. As Jesus walked on this earth, he didn't demand people come to him, he found them. He is relevant to our needs. "And my God will fully satisfy every need of yours according to his riches in glory in Christ Jesus" (Philippians 4:19). Jesus truly considers the needs of his customers and exceeds our expectations every time.

Find a Need and Fill It

Peter Drucker in *Managing the Nonprofit Organization* describes the changing face of museums.

> Museums . . . used to see themselves as cultural custodians. Their administrators believed in keeping art in and people out. Most museums today work hard to create customers for taste, for beauty, and for inspiration. They see themselves as educational institutions.[4]

Are our churches custodians of tradition, or are they about mission? Martin Luther warned that each generation should be careful not to make the way to the cross through the doors of their tradition. Are we about preserving our particular culture or meeting people where they are and leading them to a relationship with Jesus Christ? To be successful in this mission today, we must assess and meet the needs of our customers.

All People's Gathering, a Lutheran church in Milwaukee, Wisconsin, is an inner city church with an African-American culture. Pastor Greg Van Dunk says worship attendance was in decline and eventually declined to zero. They determined the literacy of the people in the area was quite low, so they redesigned worship services with that sensitivity and with music of that culture. With these changes and innovative leadership development programs, the attendance at worship is again on the rise.

WHICH NEEDS WILL YOU FILL?

Once you have identified all your customers and have identified each customer's needs, the difficult question is, "to which customers will we provide service?"

It is very difficult to attempt to meet all the needs of all the customers. Many churches have their hands full with just the customers they currently have. Adding more customers and filling their needs will require resources greater than they possess. The key is to match the gifts, talents, abilities, and culture of the church to the greatest customer needs, and then focus on quality in that area. As quality is applied, the waste and deficiencies of the program are eliminated, which in turn result in greater time and resources to apply to additional customers. A growing ministry results in growing resources. Quality management of those resources allows expansion of the customer base to reach even more customers. You begin to find more needs to fill while the ministry grows with quality. Take time to explore the techniques and tools that have been developed for identifying customers and their needs. You will find that those resources can be helpful in identifying which customers to initially target and what needs you will attempt to fill first.

Peachtree Presbyterian Church is in Atlanta, Georgia. Dr. Frank Harrington studied his community and found a need for an athletic program. He hired an athletic director and established programs to meet that need. As a result, attendance in those programs grew to over 2000, and many people have experienced transformation in their lives.

Many congregations have discovered the 20/80 rule. That is, 20 percent of the population contributes 80 percent of the effort. It may be 20 percent of the members contribute 80 percent of the offering. It may be 20 percent of the people contribute 80 percent of the volunteer time. Businesses often refer to this as the Pareto principle. Many businesses rely on a few customers to receive the majority of their products. This has also been referred to as the Vital Few/Useful Many principle. While there may be many customers, as a group they do not provide the significant business. Most businesses will continue to try to reach more customers while putting significant effort in keeping their vital few. It is helpful for congregations to analyze their customers from this viewpoint. While this may not affect all the programs and services, it may be helpful in designing a stewardship program or in seeking volunteers or in determining which customer needs you will meet.

QUICK

A young woman arrived at her new place of employment. She was hired to be the church's new youth director. Full of excitement about the future possibilities, she set out to meet and get to know the youth. The program was in disarray, so she planned an event announcing to the congregation that a new program has started and asking them to come meet their new director.

However, she was told that she could not make this decision on her own; the event would first need to be approved by the church council. They were scheduled to meet in three weeks and this topic would be added to that agenda. The probable outcome was the referral of the proposal to the youth committee, which would meet the following month. Their report would be presented at the next council meeting the following month. A decision on this event would possibly be given then.

The traditional church hierarchy supports power and authority at the top. Control is maintained over the entire process. This is an extremely slow management system and certainly does not provide quick responsiveness to needs. Many corporations today are moving from this system to a system that places more authority and decision-making power at the levels closest to the process. A youth director should be able to make decisions concerning the youth program.

Some churches confuse discussion with decision. Most decisions could be made quickly without a lot of discussion. Some topics are talked to death. Meanwhile, needs go unfulfilled. Providing a *quick* responsiveness to needs may require churches to examine their governance structure.

CUSTOMER RELATIONS

We now ask the question, "How are you managing the relationships with your customers?"

Every member of your staff, every volunteer, every leader in your congregation is a member of your customer relations team. The person who maintains your grounds and facilities may be the first person a new customer meets when visiting your facility. A church volunteer may be the first to spot the motorist with the flat tire. Training all staff, volunteers, and leaders in customer relations is necessary. All must see themselves as interacting with customers.

The persons who regularly come into contact with your customers can be called customer contact people. All churches, regardless of size, have people that fit into this group. They may be receptionists, custodians, grounds keepers, traffic control volunteers, ushers, or greeters. In addition to paid staff, they may be volunteers working in the office, answering the telephone, or serving in any other number of ways. How are these people trained to be your congregation's ambassador to your customer?

Saint Paul wrote to the Colossians, "Whatever your task, put your-
selves into it, as done for the Lord and not for your masters, since you
know that from the Lord you will receive the inheritance as your reward;
you serve the Lord Christ" (Colossians 3:23-24).

How would an usher at your church act if he or she saw Jesus coming
for worship? Would Jesus be warmly welcomed with a smile? Would Jesus
be given help in finding a seat, and would someone make sure all his needs
were filled? How would your receptionist sound on the phone if he or she
knew Jesus was the one calling?

Indeed, Jesus is the one we are serving. He said, "Truly I tell you, just
as you did it to one of the least of these who are members of my family,
you did it to me" (Matthew 25:40).

Many congregations assign the task of customer relations solely to the
pastor. Along with being the welcoming committee on Sunday, he or she is
the one to make all visits to members, visitors, shut-ins, hospitals, and
lapsed members. This is a responsibility to be shared. Volunteers trained
and gifted in care ministry can make effective and meaningful calls. This is
rewarding to the volunteer and visited person alike.

We have recently opened a part-time staff position in the area of guest
relations. This position puts the greatest focus on serving our first-time visitors. But we also attempt to serve all other customers and to nurture
relationships with them.

How are you doing in the area of customer relations? Are you getting
repeat visitors or losing 90 percent of them? Are your new people being
assimilated into the life of the congregation? Are your worship attenders
participants or spectators? Are your members attending regularly, or are
there large gaps between visits? What are your hours of business? Are you
available for customer calls? Do you have visitor packets available for your
first-time visitors so that they can learn more about your ministry?
Resources are available to help churches become more hospitable places.
Check with your national church body or publisher.

Jesus did not come to be served but to serve.

Total Quality Ministry Improves Your Serve

CUSTOMER FOCUS

The key to keeping the customer focus is to place the customer's needs
ahead of those of the organization.

People Are Always the Priority

Is your ministry focused on your customer? Are you more sensitive to his or her needs than your own needs? A common misconception here is that a church needs to have a single focus. Just as there are multiple customers for each church, there may be multiple areas of focus. In each focus area, it is essential to target the needs of the customer, not the needs of the organization. A still camera takes one picture. The subject of the picture is the area of focus. The background may be blurry and other things may be included but not in focus. A video or movie constantly has the subject of each frame in focus although the subject may change. A church that sees it has many customers will learn to keep each frame in focus.

Frequently, Sunday morning becomes a time for congregational leaders to carry on the "business" of the church. One Sunday following the morning worship, one of the council members approached Walt and started discussing some building repairs that needed to be done. While he was talking, Walt noticed a first-time guest with a tear streaming down her face. By the time he was able to break away from the well-intentioned council member, the guest had disappeared. Fortunately, she returned three weeks later to give Community Church of Joy another chance. While both the woman and the council member are customers, needs should be prioritized so that the needs of the organization always take a second place to the personal needs of customers. How is the atmosphere conditioned always to place the needs of the customer ahead of the needs of the organization?

Is your church friendly to all customers? *User Friendly Churches*[5] by George Barna provides great insight to those churches that have the customer in focus. Most churches believe, and will tell you, that they are friendly churches, but many have not actually evaluated themselves for friendliness through the eye of those attending. Are your worship services friendly to first-time visitors? Do you have adequate signs directing visitors? Is your terminology friendly?

We were frequently referring to the "Great Room" in our Family Life Center. Then we discovered that many of our new visitors had no idea where or what it was. We need to continuously evaluate our terminology to ensure it makes sense to all customers.

Customer focus also means placing the highest priority on guest relations. The Disney corporation is one benchmark and standard in the area of guest relations. While they are flexible with employees in many areas of employment, they will not tolerate an employee being discourteous to a guest. An employee may be terminated on the spot for this violation. At

Community Church of Joy, we have instituted a SMILE strategy to help place a premium priority on our guest relations. All staff and volunteers receive training in using this strategy as part of our guest relations focus.

S *mile*—a smile goes a long way in creating a friendly atmosphere. Whether it is the volunteer helping to park cars or the usher collecting the offering, the person is encouraged to present a smile and warm countenance.

M *eaningful touch*—an appropriate touch communicates warmth, caring, and concern. It shows interest and attention.

I *nviting attitude*—invite and encourage persons to attend events; show the way to the classroom; encourage participation.

L *isten*—communicate caring and concern by really listening to the other person. You cannot be listening when you are talking.

E *ye contact*—this communicates focused attention on the customer.

Is your ministry healthy or unhealthy in keeping the focus on the customer and not on the institution? Keeping the focus on the needs of the customer builds trust, confidence, respect, and community. These are essential for ministry.

CUSTOMER SATISFACTION

How friendly and focused on the customer are you? We may have our impressions, but only the customer knows for sure. Chapter 3 will discuss several performance measurement techniques to help determine the satisfaction of your customer. The importance here is to use measurable data and actual facts to back up your evaluation. The impression you or your leadership has on your focus may not be clear.

Never Assume It—Assess It

Use the measurement tools and the assessment tools listed previously to measure the gap between customer expectations and your church's performance, and then reduce that gap.

Studies have shown that a satisfied customer will tell a few people about their positive experience; a dissatisfied customer will tell 19 others about their negative experience.

To be effective and keep good customer relations, quick action needs to be taken on all feedback. If a customer has a complaint, he or she needs to know that not only is the complaint heard, but also that action will be taken to correct the situation. Then the customer waits to see how long it takes. If it takes too long, we have lost credibility. The management of feedback becomes important to a ministry with a customer focus.

For some businesses, the staff or volunteer person who first discovers or hears of a problem "owns" the problem. It is that person's responsibility to either take corrective action, organize the necessary team of persons who can effectively deal with the problem, or to make sure that the problem is delivered to the proper person who has the authority and responsibility to take action. The importance here is that the problem is not lost through persons who say it is not their job to fix it. Feedback should then be given to the customer who first experienced the problem.

COMPETITION

In the discussion of the customer, the subject of competition needs to be addressed. In the business community, competitors are those who are trying to market to the same people with similar products or services. If it is assumed that there is a finite market, each business is competing for the greatest market share. Many businesses will go to extreme lengths to out-do their competition to win market share.

In the Christian church, we should also take a close look at our competition. (We are assuming a congregation is interested in gaining new members.) If we are a Lutheran church that is focused and targeted on gaining Lutherans, we will be in competition with the nearest Lutheran church that has the same target. We will be seeking our market share of Lutherans. If we are a Christian church targeting Christians, we will be in competition with other congregations that are also targeting Christians. Some congregations may not be actively seeking market share, but we do know that some people will shop for their services between churches. These people may attend a small group in one church, worship in another, and have their children in the youth group at still another. (Some claim to be giving their money at one of the other churches.) In these circumstances, we are in competition.

If, however, our target is the unchurched, then we are on the same team as other congregations. We celebrate the successes of each other. There is more than enough of a market for all of us. Our competition is not another Christian church just down the street or across the corner. There is no room in mission for jealousy nor for unfair judgment. Whereas success sometimes breeds contempt, judgments should never precede a thorough evaluation. Our competition comes from those activities or attitudes that keep people out of our churches.

The competition may be sports activities, it may be travel, it may be television, it may be indifference, it may be shopping malls, it may be cults, it may be a previous bad experience in the church.

Competition Is Whatever Keeps People Away from Our Churches and Outside God's Kingdom

Time is increasingly becoming a competitor for churches.

It appears that the claims about Americans being increasingly likely to give their time to worthy organizations may be overblown. . . . the enormous demands on people's time are draining them of the energy and opportunity to offer their time as freely as in the past. Overall, there is a net loss noted in the proportion of people who say they are volunteering more time this year than last. . . . The bad news for churches is that across-the-board people are spending less time participating in church activities.[6]

CONGREGATIONAL SELF-ASSESSMENT

How well does this congregation provide for its customers who seek assistance, need directions, have questions or comments, have complaints, or identify special needs? How visitor friendly is the campus? Would a new visitor or a vendor easily find his or her way around? Use this continuum to rate your congregation.

1	2	3	4	5	6	7	8	9	10

No   Some   Excellent
Programs   Provisions   Signs and Help

How well does this congregation assess its overall performance through the eyes of its customers? Are the customers satisfied with the services provided? How do you know?

1	2	3	4	5	6	7	8	9	10

No   Occasional   Frequent
Provisions   Feedback   Customer Assessment

PRACTICAL APPLICATION

With your leadership team, conduct a self-evaluation using these questions as a guide. In your context or setting:

1. Who are your customers?
2. How does your ministry reflect the societal and demographic makeup of your community, and how are you meeting the needs of these people?
3. What are the most important factors in maintaining and building relationships with your customers?
4. What specific training do your customer-contact people receive?
5. How do you make it easy for customers to comment both positively and negatively?
6. Who is your competition? How can you compete against those things that keep people out of your church? Do you understand this competition?

The **Q** in quality is Quick Responsiveness to Needs. The next chapter will focus on the **U** in Quality.

Chapter 3

Q
U nity of Purpose
A
L
I
T
Y

When Walt first arrived at Community Church of Joy in 1978, most of the leaders had a wonderful plan for the ministry. One leader told Walt that the reason the church called him was to spend a lot of time relating to teenagers. Another Council member said that the most important part of his job was to visit every member in their home every year. (Since we had less than 100 families, that wasn't impossible.) Still another leader told him that his job was to teach numerous Bible classes.

Those were all important parts of ministry. However, what was clearly missing was a unity of purpose. Doing many great things couldn't be ignored, but the questions that really needed answers were:

- Why are we doing this or that program?
- How can this best be accomplished?
- What is the purpose of this ministry?
- What has God called this congregation to do or to be?

The answers to these questions are determined by the purpose of the mission. On a retreat with leaders about a year after Walt arrived, a mission statement was crafted. Then an effective strategy to do the best job possible in carrying out this purpose was designed.

Once we were united around our purpose and mission, the church became more effective, efficient, and excellent in ministry.

The process of Total Quality Ministry taken from the corporate world of Total Quality Management has many applications to the Christian church. The corporate model is lacking in the important area of ministry. The corporate model is two-dimensional, if you will, in that it seeks the customers needs and seeks to fill those needs in a quality manner. The two-dimensional aspect is the supply and demand.

The *third dimension* in Total Quality Ministry is that ministry seeks not only to identify the customer's needs and then meet the needs with quality, but also to *transform* the life of the customer with the power of the gospel.

The Third Dimension Is Transformation

A fast-food restaurant may seek to provide the best hamburgers to keep you as a repeat customer. It does not seek to change its customers into steak lovers, nor does it seek to provide great steaks.

A church seeks to meet the needs of the first-time visitor who may be a nonchurched person. Through the efforts of the ministry, the person is encouraged and led in the walk of maturation of faith through the work of the Holy Spirit. As the person takes this path, transformation occurs. The ministry then must respond to the transformed person. While the corporate world is challenged to meet the changing needs of its customers, the Christian community encourages its customers to be transformed and then must be prepared to respond to those new creations. The Bible says it best, "So if anyone is in Christ, there is a new creation: everything old has passed away; see, everything has become new!" (2 Corinthians 5:17).

This third dimension of Total Quality is not found in the literature for the corporate world. We summarize it here in terms of *mission* and *mission strategy.*

MISSION

It sometimes seems that everyone has a wonderful plan for your church. Each of your members knows what the church should be and will tell you so. For some, church is a nice place for social or business connections. Others believe the church is a good place to go when you get in trouble. Others believe church is where you are baptized, married, and buried. People will always tell you what they think the pastor should be doing, and he or she probably cannot do it all. But do you know why you are in ministry? What has God called you to do? Who has God called you to be?

Through the work of strategic planning, you can determine the direction you are to take and what unifies all the differing areas of your ministry.

Jesus prayed for unity for the disciples in his prayer before he was betrayed (John 17). As he sent them and us into the world, Jesus said "Go therefore and make disciples of all nations, baptizing them in the name of the Father and of the Son and of the Holy Spirit, and teaching them to obey everything that I have commanded you" (Matthew 28:19-20). This gives us our unifying direction. We share a common vision and mission. The unity does not mean uniformity. We can be united in purpose while celebrating diversity and creativity. Just as an orchestra is made of many parts and each instrument plays its separate notes, when played together under expert guidance the result is spectacular.

Unity Is Harmonized Diversity

For each congregation, there must be a central theme that ties all efforts together. It is true that if you don't know where you are going, any road will get you there. To find out where you are going or where you should be going and how you are to get there, quality plans must be developed.

Quality plans begin with the most basic of questions: What has God called us to do?

The answer to this question leads to the formation of a mission statement. The mission statement does not come from just any elected or appointed committee of members. It is developed through the inspiration of the Holy Spirit in mature members who are earnestly seeking that inspiration. It needs to be developed through the involvement of the spiritual leaders of the congregation.

The mission statement for Community Church of Joy is the following:

That all may know Jesus Christ and become responsible members of his Church, we share his love with joy inspired by the Holy Spirit.

This is the answer to what God has called Community Church of Joy to do. It is the guide and filter for decision, direction, and strategy. It is memorized by our leaders and displayed in various ways on the campus, i.e., on Sunday worship bulletins, on banners, on church board meeting agendas, and so forth. It is the topic of the Sunday message several times each year. The average person will forget your mission unless it is repeated many times and repeated in many creative ways. Our mission continuously reminds us that there are many who do not yet know Jesus Christ, and there is much work to do. It also reminds us that we are responsible for making disciples, and the way to make disciples is in sharing the love of Christ.

STRATEGY

Strategy answers the question of how the mission is to be accomplished. Each congregation must develop its strategy after determining its mission.

For Community Church of Joy, the strategy to accomplish our mission follows an illustration from baseball. While no analogy can be perfect, it does provide us an aid for leadership, understanding, and direction. The object in winning the game is to score runs. To do so requires the batter to reach each base safely and then move on to the next. If a person never goes beyond first base, she or he cannot score. If a person never reaches home plate, no runs are scored.

First base is *Celebration*. Celebration includes worship services and outreach events such as concerts, dramas, special dynamic speakers, or any other presentation that intentionally reaches out to the congregation and community. We seek to help first time and repeat customers reach first base. There is success in this step but it is not the end point.

Second base is *Growth*. The Christian life is dynamic; it is not static. Either we are growing, or we are dying. On second base, growth takes place through a Bible study, a small group discussion, a seminar, a retreat, a class, or numerous other training and equipping opportunities. Maturing Christians move on to third base.

Third base is *Prayer & Care*. Great mission requires prayer. Prayer plugs us in to the power that propels magnificent mission. This base includes prayer concerts, prayer vigils, prayer team training, prayer groups, intercessory networks, and prayer retreats, classes, and seminars. Third base also includes Care. People being served with Prayer & Care are encouraged, healed, and enriched. We train and develop persons who are equipped to assist in prayer and care ministries.

The runs are scored when a person reaches home plate. Home plate is *Missions*. It is here that we sacrificially serve. It is here that hungry people are fed, homeless people are given shelter, sick people are given a healing touch, lonely people have a friend, thirsty people have their thirst quenched, injustice is ended, orphans are given a family, and widows and widowers are given new hope. At home plate, faith is put into action.

The two dimensions of corporate quality are meeting the needs of the customer through the exchange of a product or service for a compensation. The *third dimension* of quality ministry meets the needs of the person on first base, encourages him or her to move to second base and meets his or her needs there. In summary, the third dimension produces lives that are transformed through Jesus Christ.

Community Church of Joy has adopted this strategy for the overall ministry as well as individual ministries. The youth ministry uses this strategy. By providing opportunities for celebration and outreach events, youth are encouraged toward first base. Small groups and youth education opportunities are available for second base, and so on. The same is true for adult education, singles, and for each area of ministry.

VISION

Pastor John Maxwell of Skyline Wesleyan in San Diego, California, has said,

If There Is Hope in the Future, There Is Power in the Present

The question, "Who has God called us to be as this congregation?" is answered in the vision statement. Vision is a statement of how the organization will look, act, and minister at some point in the future. The mature and visionary leadership of the congregation may participate in the development of the vision statement. It is a conceptual plan with little detail but addresses most areas of ministry focus. It demonstrates how the mission will remain in focus for years to come and should look at least five years, but not more than ten years, into the future.

The vision is developed by the leadership so that it will receive the promotion and consideration deserved. It is the guide for major long-range and short-range planning and decision making. It is where the leadership of the congregation must be years ahead of the congregation.

Vision Is Not Based on Present Reality
But on Future Possibilities

In 1984, Walt saw the future possibilities that were a part of the vision for Community Church of Joy. He knew that the present property would not be big enough to accomplish this vision. He communicated well, but it wasn't until 1986 that Steve also saw this vision. The vision was communicated to the board of directors, and in 1988, the whole board saw and internalized this vision. In 1992, the congregation of Community Church of Joy saw and embraced this vision. In 1994, the land was ours. As demonstrated, leadership must lead in the vision.

The accomplishment of a vision doesn't always require buildings or relocation. We've already seen what vision did for All People's Gathering in Milwaukee. The vision to meet the needs of people in new ways, where they already are, may be what God is calling you to do.

The vision statement is prepared best in a retreat-like context where sufficient uninterrupted time is available for prayer, dreaming, and discussion. Demographic data (discussed in Chapter 2) is available to help guide the discussion.

All leaders are asked through prayer to express their dreams and desires of what the congregation could be in ten years. What could it be doing? What is the Lord seeking to accomplish in this congregation in the next ten years? The answers will be in general terms with few specifics. Finances are not a constraint for any dream, although finances need to be planned as well. In order to keep the creative flow of ideas, it may be necessary to prevent any "dream killers" from making value judgments on any of the ideas expressed at this time.

The dreams and insights may be categorized and summarized. Community Church of Joy leaders developed categories such as leadership, education, facilities, relationships, finances, staffing, and others.

Next, a cursory "reality check" should be made with respect to whether the dreams are supported by the demographic data. A ministry to senior citizens is difficult in an area without seniors. Do the dreams match the strengths and mission of the congregation? Encouraging the dreams before doing the reality check helps to open possibilities rather than restrict ideas.

Each area of the vision is then developed into more specifics, called objectives. For each objective category, such as leadership, specific goals are listed that must be attained to achieve the vision. Next, action plans are developed. These may be one-, three-, or five-year plans and are even more specific and directed. The action plans are prepared or updated annually as part of the quality improvement plan. These action plans are then deployed into the ministry areas as specific, directed actions and goals for the year.

Each year an evaluation is conducted to determine whether the actions and goals for that year have been met and where the ministry is in meeting the objectives. In addition, the vision is reviewed, objectives are refined, and projections are updated as more information and progress is made. This also provides feedback to the improvement policies for the coming year.

In this manner, the target is prepared some years into the future. Then, each year, the plan for reaching the target is refined, and progress made toward reaching the target is measured so that the ministry may stay on its time line. Annual decisions are focused with the vision in mind. Steps are taken toward that vision each day, month, and year until the vision is achieved. Before that happens, new dreams and visions should be under development.

While it would be difficult in one step to make the change from where we are today to where we want to be ten years from now, knowing that there are ten years ahead allows us to dream with greater possibilities. While finances should not determine the course of the ministry, the ministry plans will determine what finances are needed to accomplish the vision. Plans can then be prepared for financial development as well.

VALUES

The values are the beliefs and standards that underlie the vision, mission, and strategy. They set the guidelines by which action plans are designed. They help to express the area of greatest importance to the internal customers of staff and volunteers.

Community Church of Joy developed its value statements as follows:

THE GOSPEL

We value a Lutheran understanding of the Gospel. A commitment to the Word alone, Faith alone, and Grace alone undergirds and shapes our ministry that Jesus Christ might be exalted as Savior and Lord.

PEOPLE

We value the God-given worth of each individual. We exist to help them discover their God-given potential through a relationship with Jesus Christ and to help them grow as his disciples. We will treat all people with dignity and respect, and we will continually build a climate of warmth, acceptance, and hospitality.

STAFF

We value the uniqueness and special gifts of each staff member. The staff is our greatest asset, and we will work together to value each other and to bring out the best in one another.

OUTREACH

We value a relevant, practical, theologically correct, life-transforming presentation of the Gospel. Because lost people matter to God, we will continue to find ways to connect with them that they might be able to consider the claims of Christ in an atmosphere of openness and encouragement.

PRAYER

We value prayer as the power for effective mission and ministry.

EXCELLENCE

We value excellence, efficiency, effectiveness, and quality in every area of ministry, knowing that joy comes from doing our best.

INTEGRITY

We value honesty, openness, fairness, and grace in dealing with one another. We will continually encourage one another to excel in integrity in all areas, especially in the management of time, talent, people, and finances.

INNOVATION

We will create an environment which encourages bold dreams, innovation, risk taking, and the freedom to fail, that we might be more effective in the mission of the church.

Each congregation in its own context should be empowered to determine its own set of value statements.

STRATEGIC QUALITY PLANNING

Until recently, few American corporations included quality in their strategic planning. Total Quality Management changed that. In a like manner, congregations should include quality improvement as part of the strategic plan. Each annual improvement policy should include the quality improvement goals along with other ministry goals. As we seek to deliver ministry to the customer with excellence, we should seek continuous improvement in that delivery.

As manufacturers produce a product, they may measure defects or deficiencies in the product and seek ways to reduce the number of defects. In ministry, we must admit we have our deficiencies. When a person arrives at a schedule room for a particular class and the class is not meeting there, it is a deficiency to be corrected. Whether the failure occurred in promotion, facilities, cancellation, or for whatever reason, the needs of the customer have not been met. This deficiency should not be ignored, and plans should be developed instead to address the deficiency. If we honestly evaluate our ministry, we will find areas of deficiency. Action plans need to be implemented to bring about continuous improvement.

> The nonprofits are human-change agents. And their results are therefore always a change in people—in their behavior, in their circumstances, in their vision, in their health, in their hopes, above all, in their competence and capacity. In the last analysis, the nonprofit institution . . . has to judge itself by its performance in creating vision, creating standards, creating values and commitment, and in creating human competence. The nonprofit institution therefore needs to set specific goals in terms of its service to people. And it needs constantly to raise these goals—or its performance will go down.[1]

CONGREGATIONAL SELF-ASSESSMENT

Based on the mission, vision, and strategy of this congregation, has this congregation completed long-range strategic planning? Does this congregation have a view of its future potential? Does it know what steps will be necessary to achieve this potential? Have these plans been documented? Use this continuum to rate your congregation.

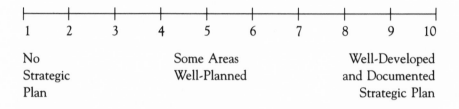

| 1 | 2 | 3 | 4 | 5 | 6 | 7 | 8 | 9 | 10 |

No
Strategic
Plan

Some Areas
Well-Planned

Well-Developed
and Documented
Strategic Plan

How effectively are the mission, vision, strategy, and strategic planning utilized by the leadership and management of this congregation to promote unity of purpose? Are these important documents actual guidelines for decisions and resource allocations, or are they simply decorations on a shelf? Does the leadership believe in this mission and vision? How well is this congregation developing leaders who understand and have internalized these guides?

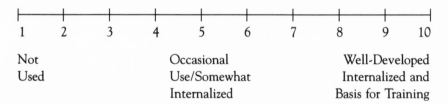

| 1 | 2 | 3 | 4 | 5 | 6 | 7 | 8 | 9 | 10 |

Not
Used

Occasional
Use/Somewhat
Internalized

Well-Developed
Internalized and
Basis for Training

© *Total Quality Ministry: Congregational Self-Assessment*, The JOY Company, 1994

PRACTICAL APPLICATION

With the leadership of your congregation, answer the following questions.

1. State your mission statement from memory. If you do not have a mission statement, make that your first goal and create an action plan to develop it.

2. Do you have a written three-, five-, or ten-year strategic quality plan? If not, make this another goal, and create an action plan to develop it.
3. What is your strategy to carry out your mission? Discuss your values. Do your staff and volunteers know them?
4. How should the congregational leaders be trained and educated in the mission, vision, strategy, values, and strategic planning so that all can have the same focus in decision making?

Quick Responsiveness to Needs and Unity of Purpose are the **QU** in Quality. The next chapter focuses on the **A** in Quality.

Chapter 4

Q
U
A nticipation and Expectation
L
I
T
Y

A young imaginative pastor moved into a community where the average age was 27 years old. There were children everywhere. This pastor wanted to connect with the people in her community in the best possible way. As Pastor Jane listened to the needs of young parents, she developed a seminar for toilet training.

When Jane was putting the seminars together, she invited a local child psychologist to team teach with her. In her publicity, she wanted to include a Bible verse. She decided on "Train a child in the way he [she] should go . . ." (Proverbs 22:6 RSV). Everyone had a good laugh and the seminar was a smashing success.

Jane anticipated a real need and exceeded the expectations of those who participated. Because the seminar was so successful, many of the participants actually ended up becoming members of the church. Anticipation and expectation is an essential ingredient to a quality ministry.

*F*or several hundred years the Israelites lived with the promise of God that they would have a land of their own. It had been promised to Abraham, Isaac, and Jacob. Now the promise was renewed with Moses. As they stood just outside Canaan, Moses sent spies into the land. He must have waited with great expectation for the spies to return. When they did, ten of the twelve spread a bad report. Only two of the twelve (20 percent) believed that with God, all things are possible.

The Israelites missed their opportunity, and for most it was truly an opportunity of a lifetime. Many must have believed that the timing of the fulfillment of God's promise was not right, or maybe they even questioned whether the promise was true. Many may not have even realized that this was their opportunity after all these years. That was the failure of their expectation and anticipation. They were not expecting much, nor were they ready to receive God's promise when it was offered.

Expectation and anticipation go beyond wishful thinking to assurance that something will happen. The confidence becomes so strong that courageous plans are made on the outcome.

Your customers have an expectation of quality related to the services and programs provided. You anticipate the results to be achieved through the introduction of a new ministry service or program. Planning quality into the formation of that new ministry service can help you achieve the anticipated results and meet the customers' expectations.

QUALITY OF PROGRAMS AND SERVICES

The quality of programs and services are part of the initial formation of the plans for those programs and services. That is, the quality of the program is designed and considered before the service is begun.

There are three quality processes involved in any ministry program or service. Referred to as the Juran Trilogy, they are quality planning, quality control, and quality improvement.[1]

Quality planning is involved in the starting point discussions for programs or ministry. The program is planned with the principles of total quality in mind. *Quality control* is the on-going monitoring of the delivery of that program or service to ensure that its delivery remains consistent with the total quality principles. *Quality improvement* reviews the quality of the program delivered, compares it to that which was planned, and determines how that service or ministry may be improved in the future.

Frequently, we in the church spend much of our time in the quality control area trying to make sure things don't get worse. Our efforts don't always get translated into resolving the original problem, and the same deficiencies return.

Recently a psychologist referred to a dysfunctional family situation as one where there is broken glass all over the floor. Everyone is hurt while stepping on the glass. One person in that family may try to carefully step where there is no glass in order to avoid the pain. Another person may try to sweep up the glass to avoid pain for the whole family. Eventually, it is necessary to stop the breaking of the glass.

This concept is one of the major paradigm shifts for manufacturing companies today. In years past, the quality of a product was determined to be acceptable if a statistical sampling of products at the end of the process passed the final inspection. That was quality based on inspection and is what companies traditionally called "quality control." Unfortunately, the defective products that were not sampled were found by the customer. Expectations were not met and costs were high. Today, companies are finding ways to eliminate potential sources of deficiencies in the process before the process is even built, and they are also finding ways to quickly determine whether the process is breaking down.

Quality control helps to keep the broken glass picked up. Quality improvement seeks to stop the breaking of the glass. Most businesses have recognized that the paradigm has shifted from the detection of errors through quality control to the prevention of errors through quality planning.

Quality planning means the starting point is the customer. Your new service or program is based on meeting a specific need of a customer or group of customers. You develop the features of the new program to meet the needs of the customer. Along with the features, you plan the quality measurements you will use to measure the effectiveness and resulting customer satisfaction with this new ministry program. After deciding on the features, you plan the process of delivering those features. You add the quality measurement features that will ensure the delivery meets the customer expectations. Finally, you plan the quality measurement features you will use to measure the customer satisfaction with the service provided. All this is done *before* the service is provided.

Suppose you are approached to present an adult class on stress and what the Bible teaches about stress. Quality by design requires a complete and thorough look at all aspects of this process before the class starts. You will want to consider these questions.

- How large is the need for this class?
- Is it truly a customer need?
- Is it a need that promotes your vision and mission?
- What is the material to be presented?
- Who can prepare an informative, theologically correct, caring interpretation of this subject?

- How is the quality checked before the class is advertised?
- Who has the gift of teaching to present this material?
- Has this teacher been evaluated by knowledgeable people?
- How long should classes run? How many sessions should there be?
- Is it better held as a longer seminar? Are there potential conflicts?
- How is the class to be advertised?
- Is the planning thorough enough to avoid cancellation or changes in the schedule?
- If changes need to be made, how will that be communicated to potential customers?
- Are the classrooms checked to be appropriate for this discussion?
- How do you make sure the teacher will have all the materials necessary?
- Are the printed materials checked for completeness and accuracy prior to the class?
- How do you anticipate the number of participants so that you can ensure an adequate supply of materials?
- How will you evaluate the performance of the teacher?
- How will you know whether this service met the need first identified?

These questions and many others must be answered prior to the start of the class. Frequently we may find ourselves preparing to teach a class only to discover that the overhead projector is not in the room. Time is wasted searching for it. The teacher picked to lead the class may be able to present the material but is not knowledgeable enough to answer the questions. A thorough planning effort for quality in the design of the service avoids the costly problems that lead to customer dissatisfaction that could occur if the service is not properly planned.

Failure to Plan Means the Failures Are Planned

We are responsible for the failures that occur, especially if we have not considered the possible failures when we planned the service. We are familiar with the saying that people do not plan to fail, they fail to plan. In like manner, each failure in the process of delivering a service or program is likely the result of failures in the planning process. The quality improvement phase then seeks to take each failure and plan out its recurrence in the next cycle.

Pastor Larry Smooze of God's Love Lutheran Church, in New Town Pennsylvania, reported that every event they hold is evaluated. By doing so, they discover that the way it was conducted may not always be the best way. This tells them how to improve on the next event. Leaders evaluate the effectiveness of the event in terms of whether or not the mission was accomplished.

These quality processes are frequently described in the Plan-Do-Check-Act cycle. The program is planned with quality; it is implemented; the process is checked and evaluated; and the results are actions for improvement. It is a cycle in that the actions are part of the planning of the next program. That program is then implemented, checked, and its results evaluated in terms of what improvements can be made. Thus the cycle continues. Each cycle eliminates the failures of the previous cycle so that errors are not repeated, time is not lost in putting out fires, customers are more satisfied, and those involved in the process take greater pride and ownership of the product delivered.

Dr. Robert Schuller says he has a new bumper sticker. It reads

If It Works, Don't Fix It, Improve It

At times, even the best plans develop deficiencies. The Hubble Space Telescope is a prime and costly example. A flaw 1/50th the width of a hair causes blurring of some images. There is no question of the engineering and care that went into the original manufacture of the mirror. Nevertheless, the goals of the Hubble Space Telescope required servicing of the telescope in space.

In *Dying for Change*,[2] Leith Anderson identifies several steps in the decision-making process for change. This also has application in the Plan-Do-Check-Act cycle.

1. *Define the Issue.* Actually get to the root of the problem or deficiency.
2. *Get the Facts.* Assemble the facts so that those involved in the decision process can be as objective as possible.
3. *Consider the Alternatives.* Identify all possible solutions.
4. *Make the Decision.* The person or person(s) authorized to make the decision are identified in advance, if possible, but the decision must be made at this point.
5. *Do It!* A change is not a change until it is implemented and action is taken.

The balance of the cycle is then to monitor the process, check the results, and act on those results for improvement.

Performance in the nonprofit institution must be planned. And this starts out with the mission. Nonprofits fail to perform unless they start out with their mission. For the mission defines what results are in this particular nonprofit institution. . . . One of the basic differences between businesses and nonprofits is that nonprofits always have a multitude of constituencies. . . . The success of the growing pastoral churches largely depends on their realizing that the needs of young people, young married couples, singles, and older people are different. The church has to set a performance goal with respect to each group and use competent individuals who can deliver performance.[3]

BENCHMARKS

Churches that may be doing a particular ministry or program well provide us a benchmark. A benchmark provides the standard or goal to which we can aspire. Knowing that others have actually achieved this standard gives direction to those who may have a similar service. While businesses view a benchmark as an objective in order to beat the competition, churches may view a benchmark as a goal for quality improvement. In the corporate world, each business will guard its secrets and processes to maintain its competitive edge. In the Christian church, ideas and successes and failures are shared with others for overall improvement.

The benefits of competitive benchmarking include the following items.

- Creating a culture that values continuous improvement to achieve excellence.
- Enhancing creativity by devaluing the "not-invented-here" syndrome.
- Increasing sensitivity to changes in the external environment.
- Shifting the corporate (congregation) mindset from relative complacency to a strong sense of urgency for ongoing improvement.
- Focusing resources through performance targets jointly set with employees.
- Prioritizing the areas to work on first.
- Sharing the best practices between benchmarking partners.[4]

Some churches become teaching churches to assist others through the same struggles and successes. Lyle Schaller, noted church consultant, has said that the teaching church is the key learning center of the future. It is the laboratory of testing and discovery of "cutting edge," creative, and innovative ministry. Some churches that have assumed the role of being a teaching church include Willow Creek Community in Barrington, Illinois; Saddleback Community Church in Mission Viejo, California; as well as Community Church of Joy in Glendale, Arizona. Many churches are beginning to teach other churches in their local area or are teaching specific subjects for which they have established benchmark ministries.

As Christian churches work in harmony, the teaching church has a responsibility to share with others the lessons learned. There will be a cost in doing so in the areas of staff time, materials, phone calls, and ongoing education, so those resources must be developed.

PERFORMANCE INDICATORS

As we have planned our programs and services, we started with our mission and vision and may have used certain benchmark information as a particular goal. Checking the results of our programs and services in order to improve them is the next step. Chapter 6 will cover the statistical processes involved, but just as the economy has its leading indicators, there could be specific indicators of overall congregational performance.

1. MISSION AND VISION

As was discussed in Chapter 2, your mission states what God has called you to do. Your vision leads to strategic planning. It would seem appropriate then to evaluate your current situation with respect to your mission and your vision. Are you succeeding in achieving and doing what your mission statement says you are called to do? Have you established measurement tools necessary to evaluate your progress? Are you reaching the annual goals your congregation has set with respect to your strategic plan?

Frequently we establish goals to do "great ministry" without identifying what that means. In the Peanuts cartoon, Charles Schultz illustrated Charlie Brown as he would shoot arrows into a fence and then run up to draw a bulls-eye around them. Many churches are doing that today. It is easy to hit a target that is not measurable, but a commitment to quality improvement requires the use of measurable and comparable data and statistics.

Random Shootings Are the Most Dangerous

The mission statement of Community Church of Joy was presented in Chapter 2. It is broken down in the paragraphs that follow to illustrate how we have established criteria to measure effectiveness and direction relative to that mission.

"That all may know Jesus Christ" intentionally focuses on the non-churched. As we seek continuous growth in attendance and membership, we intentionally seek growth in the number of members who come from a nonchurched background. By surveying each new class over the past several years, we have found that 60 percent of our new members come from a nonchurched background. We monitor this percentage and watch our programming to ensure that we remain committed to our continuing focus and direction.

". . . and become responsible members of his Church" intentionally focuses on the growth and maturity of members. We have defined responsible membership to mean a commitment to the following criteria.

- Regular worship attendance
- A personal prayer and devotional life
- Growth through education or small groups
- Tithing
- Mission involvement

While we do not check income tax returns to verify tithing, we have established criteria that would indicate in measurable terms each of the above items so we can evaluate ourselves against this part of our mission.

". . . we share his love with joy, inspired by the Holy Spirit" focuses on the means of carrying out this mission. We believe in the gift of joy! An atmosphere of joy and love inspired by the Holy Spirit is contagious. We focus on relationships and, specifically, our relationship with Jesus Christ. We won't allow issues to break relationships. If a conflict occurs, we face the conflict, but our attitude will always favor the side of love and grace.

Messiah Lutheran Church in Yorba Linda, California, has established its mission statement to be "To know Christ and to make Christ known." The leaders of Messiah clearly understand and have internalized this mission. They are also seeking ways to develop measurable criteria as an evaluation tool.

Each congregation will need to develop its own measurable criteria for evaluating its performance in carrying out its own mission.

2. ATTENDANCE

St. Augustine believed that we are not called just to build churches but to fill them. Empty churches do not please God.

If we are to seriously evaluate our performance, we must look at our attendance figures. Is my congregation growing numerically? The Bible talks a lot about numbers: lost sheep, lost coin, large harvest, and so forth. God is concerned about numbers. In the parable of the great banquet in Luke Chapter 14, the master sends the servants out several times to invite people to "compel people to come in, so that my house may be filled" (Luke 14:23).

What a strong imperative is the word *compel!* A congregation that is not growing is dying. What trends do you see in your worship and education attendance? What trends do you see in your visitor attendance? Measure your current situation relative to that a year or two years ago.

3. MEMBERSHIP

Congregations have a variety of "entrance requirements" for congregational membership. For some, the change in membership will become an excellent performance indicator. It will assist, along with other indicators, in establishing an overall view of congregational performance. For other congregations, membership may not be as important. Congregations ministering to baby boomers may especially recognize a generalized trait of lack of commitment. Each congregation will need to evaluate whether this is truly a performance indicator.

4. FINANCIAL INFORMATION

While the net income of a congregation does not carry the same importance as that of a for-profit business, we cannot deny that our financial resources truly are an indicator of the health and growth of our ministries. How are your contributions this year compared to last? Each congregation will respond differently, as they have varying methods of financial support. If you try to obtain financing for construction, you can be assured that financial institutions will use this as a performance indicator for you.

5. QUALITY IMPROVEMENT

As this book is focused on continuous improvement in the ministry, it necessarily must focus on the improvement of quality as a performance indicator. The quality improvement goals and plans established in Chapter 3 provide measurable information to determine the progress being made and the improvements accomplished.

6. OTHER INDICATORS

While we have identified some potential performance indicators here, each congregation will need to establish its own indicators to evaluate its own efforts at fulfilling its mission and vision (see Chapter 6). Be careful to establish indicators that truly help to indicate overall performance. Certain activities may appear to be performance indicators when they actually measure the wrong thing.

As an example, some congregations may list the number of house calls made by a pastor as a performance indicator. The fact that a house call is made may not be promoting the mission or vision of the congregation. Dr. Frank Harrington of Peachtree Presbyterian Church tells the story of a pastor of evangelism who reported enthusiastically that he had visited the home of a family six times. When Dr. Harrington asked whether the family would be joining the church, the evangelism pastor said, "The subject never came up."

SUPPLIER QUALITY

As we evaluate our own services and our overall performance for quality, we may find that at times the quality of the service or program we provide does depend on those who may be supplying us with materials. We should, therefore, be monitoring and evaluating the performance of our vendors and suppliers. The quality of the materials and supplies provided will have a direct effect on the quality of our use of those materials and supplies. Are there competitors of the supplier whose level of quality is higher? How are you treated as their customer? Are you keeping relevant data on trends in their quality and performance?

Viewing ourselves as the customer here, we have the opportunity to improve our quality when their quality is improved. This provides us the opportunity and necessity to communicate with them and provide feedback.

CONGREGATIONAL SELF-ASSESSMENT
Does the congregational management provide ministry leaders with a blueprint for planning services and programs that will take that ministry leader through the steps necessary for a quality program? Does this plan include methods for verifying that the objectives of the service or program are met and that the customers are satisfied? Use this continuum to rate your congregation's management plan.

```
├───┼───┼───┼───┼───┼───┼───┼───┼───┤
1   2   3   4   5   6   7   8   9   10
```

No   Occasional   Well-Developed
Plan   Use by Some   Plan with Feedback
                  Leaders   Planned

How well does this congregation manage the overall delivery of a program or service? How well does this congregation integrate its support services (i.e. mailing teams, office support, nursery workers, and so on) into this delivery? Are these individuals and groups included in the planning process? Does this congregation find itself fighting fires and answering complaints frequently?

```
├───┼───┼───┼───┼───┼───┼───┼───┼───┤
1   2   3   4   5   6   7   8   9   10
```

Services   Occasionally   Well-Planned,
Are Not   Well-Planned   Organized and
Planned   in Some Areas   Developed Services

© *Total Quality Ministry: Congregational Self-Assessment*, The JOY Company, 1994

PRACTICAL APPLICATION
With your leadership team, respond to these questions.

1. What quality steps are built into your ministry or program design?
2. What performance indicators have you developed for your ministry evaluation?
3. When you provide your ministry leaders with an outline for quality planning of a new program or service, what should be included?

4. What benchmark information would you seek from other
    congregations?

Quick Responsiveness to Needs, Unity of Purpose, and Anticipation and
Expectation are the **QUA** in Quality. The next chapter focuses on the **L**
in Quality.

Chapter 5

Q
U
A
L eadership Development
I
T
Y

There is nothing more difficult to take in hand, more perilous to conduct, or more uncertain in its success, than to take the lead in the introduction of a new order of things.   Machiavelli

Pastor Barb arrived at Hope Church with unlimited hope. She knew in her heart that God had big plans for her new congregation. A stinging shock came when the church treasurer became upset with her bold and daring goals. She soon learned that the treasurer, who became the most upset about money matters, also gave the least.

Barb also observed that many of her key leaders worshiped infrequently. Other leaders were not involved in any Bible study or growth opportunities. This created a weak base of leadership upon which the congregation could build.

The solution was to develop an intentional leadership training process. When Barb did that, her leaders provided more effective visionary leadership. It is essential for every congregation serious about ministry to develop an ever-enlarging base of leaders.

Effective Leaders Are Both Courageous and Considerate

LEADERSHIP

Much has been written about leadership and leadership development. (Walt has a new book on the subject, *The Everyday, Anytime Guide to Christian Leadership*, published by Augsburg Fortress.) Leadership in this chapter will focus on the leader's ability and dedication to quality and quality improvement for the organization.

While looking ahead, Philip Crosby in his book *Completeness*, describes quality for the twenty-first century in terms of these three principles:

1. Cause employees to be successful.
2. Cause suppliers to be successful.
3. Cause customers to be successful.

The leader who understands and accomplishes these principles will be a person of exceptional ability, from whom much will be demanded. This leader is defined by Crosby as the "Centurion." The following is an excerpt describing some of these exceptional talents.

> The Centurions will have to learn how to manage so that they can deal with whatever happens, and at the same time, anticipate what is coming. . . . The Centurion is not going to have the luxury of failing as often as those in previous times. . . . In trying to describe what the Centurion will have to be doing, it is apparent that hard work will be a given. However, it will have to be work that actually accomplishes something useful. . . . The Centurion will be dealing with generations raised to know computers as a normal part of life. . . . The Centurion is going to have to become skilled in the art of personal communication. The Centurion has to deliberately build Completeness into the culture of the company so that there is a compulsion to share information. The Centurion is going to have to be like an orchestra conductor. The worklife of the Centurion will be a symphony.[1]

This is a tall order for leaders, but there can be no overstatement on the importance of leadership. In many cases leaders may not accomplish all this on their own and must learn to embrace the excellence and talent around them. Stan Gault, Chairman of the Board for Goodyear Tire and Rubber Company has said, "The winners in the future will be the companies and organizations that can harness the imagination and energy of not just a few key people, but instead can call on and use the imagination and energy of every associate, all committed to finding a better way to do more and do it with less so that all concerned will benefit." There is no room in Total Quality for power struggles and personal agendas. That is a waste of time and resources, and places the focus on individuals and not the customer. Congregational leadership must insist on the proper focus and remove the interference of individuals seeking power for their own ends. Total Quality Ministry involves people who have the mission of the congregation at heart and will use their talents and abilities to further that mission.

The leader will also be one who continuously looks for his or her own training, education, and development. This leader will not have time or energy to waste. One of the important points is that the leader is not just busy but is accomplishing the right things. Many organizations are busy and work hard—but on the wrong things.

It is not necessarily a matter of doing things right—but doing the right things and doing them well. In fact, quality improvement is often more about finding new things to do than finding new ways to do the old things.

Insanity Is to Keep Doing the Same Things in the Same Way but Expecting Different Results

CONGREGATIONAL LEADERS

It is true that the organization will never grow beyond its leaders. The call is for leaders to lead. The leader sets the climate, the vision, the standards of excellence, the expectation. If quality is important to the leader, it becomes important in the organization. If it is not important to the leader, others will lose interest too.

Moses was a visionary leader. He persuaded the Children of Israel that they should go forward toward a land of milk and honey when all they could see around them was sand. One man couldn't force a whole people to set off into the desert; he had to inspire them with his vision. He also set a personal example. When they arrived at the Red Sea, Moses said, "Here's the plan. We're going to march into the sea, the Lord will part the waters, and we'll walk through on dry land." His followers looked at the Red Sea and said to him, "You first." He went, and they followed. Being out front when the risk presents itself is part of leadership. (This story also demonstrates the value of having your boss on your side, as Moses certainly did.)[2]

True congregational leadership is not necessarily a matter of position on the governing board. Sometimes the leader is a permission giver or other individual or group of individuals who have no elected or formal power. For total quality ministry to be effective and successful, the congregational leadership needs to not only endorse but support and set the pace.

Leaders instill a sense of purpose and commitment to the organization's purpose. They enable the organization to fulfill its sense of purpose in a way that meets both individual and corporate needs. When a leader is committed sufficiently, the values and principles of quality improvement are totally internalized so that his or her behavior reflects these values. . . . Such a manager has invested considerable time and energy becoming educated about these philosophies and techniques, and leads and audits the process by which the company's thinking is transformed.[3]

There is no question that instilling a culture change in a church is a large effort. It may be costly in terms of time, finances, staff, and interpersonal relationships as change happens. Leaders that give superficial approval for the process cannot lead the change. The positive impact for ministry needs to be so internalized that leaders do lead the change.

Total Quality Ministry Leads from the Heart

The leadership also needs to have the authority to make the necessary changes. It must carry the clout and be trusted by the congregation to turn the organization upside down and inside out in order to effect the change.

Total Quality Ministry Moves a Congregation from Operating from Memory to Operating with Imagination

Some churches are hampered by elected leaders who do not have the vision or passion for the mission of the church. Many leaders are unable to see beyond their own private agendas. Such leadership needs to be changed. The governing body must be formed from committed, discipled followers of Jesus Christ. We hear many stories about congregational councils that spend their meetings discussing and arguing over the price of donuts on Sunday morning, the color of the wall paint, or placement of flowers on Easter. Such decisions could be made in less than a minute, but instead, leadership energy and resources are wasted. The leaders should be discussing vision, mission, strategic planning, and other important topics.

Many congregations are finding that the committee form of leadership is draining energy. Energy is renewed *doing* ministry not in deciding *how* ministry ought to be done. Time has become extremely valuable to people; shouldn't that time be spent involved in changing people's lives rather than sitting in committees? Leadership is responsible for the volunteer program that matches people and their gifts to areas of service.

A large church in the Minneapolis/St. Paul area held a congregational meeting where the turnout was larger than the average Sunday worship attendance. The meeting lasted longer than six hours discussing the budget. It turned into a shouting match. This is energy wasted and misdirected. Leaders need to take seriously their responsibility in properly harnessing and focusing the energy of the congregation.

Because the church members rarely grow beyond the leadership, qualification requirements were established for election to the board of directors of Community Church of Joy. In Chapter 3 we discussed the measurements necessary to evaluate performance relative to the mission statement. These same five commitments became our qualification requirements. While such requirements do not preclude private agendas, our directors are more likely to be mature in faith and open to the leading of the Holy Spirit in unity. In addition, our board is committed to quality, and it desires the improvements that quality planning and management provide.

Your church leaders do not want to be spending time talking about donuts or paint. They do so because they understand what donuts should cost, and they know how to pick paint colors. They may not know how to discuss the more important topics, such as discovering the vision and planning your future. Help them by training them in these areas, and watch them get excited!

SENIOR/SOLO PASTOR

Leadership in the area of quality ministry in the church certainly needs to include, and often rely on, the senior/solo pastor. As the senior staff person, he or she will be responsible for the actual implementation of many of the quality improvement features and processes. Without the internalization of quality within the senior/solo pastor, the passion will not be caught by others. Organizations that have tried to implement new quality goals without the senior executive's personal involvement have failed.

The commitment to quality by the senior/solo pastor and leadership team must show in attitudes and expectations, but it also must be formalized into the annual improvement policies, goals, and objectives. This quality emphasis is communicated and directed to all areas involving staff and volunteers. To be effective throughout the church, it must be initiated and supported as a top-down change.

LEADERSHIP DEVELOPMENT

Peter Drucker has said that leadership has little to do with "leadership qualities" and even less to do with "charisma." It is mundane, unromantic, and boring. Its essence is performance. Leadership is a *means*. Thus, "Leadership to what end?" is the crucial question. Effective leaders see leadership as responsibility rather than rank and privilege. An effective leader knows that she or he, and no one else, is ultimately responsible. She or he is not afraid of strength in associates and subordinates, in fact, such strength is sought out and encouraged.

Effective leaders understand their own strengths and weaknesses. They see that leading cannot be done alone, and they are not afraid to surround themselves with capable and gifted people. Leaders do not seek their own glory, rather they look for the success of the mission.

Leadership development is important because much of the process of Total Quality Ministry is learned. Training institutions need to be aware of the importance of this type of leadership and teach these techniques and processes to their students. Just as Total Quality seeks continuous improvement, the leaders seek continuous learning experiences.

Pastor Greg Van Dunk of All People's Gathering in Milwaukee (noted previously for an innovative approach to worship based on his customers), has also instituted an innovative leadership development program. As he learned about his neighborhood, he found few adults who were strong leaders. He has personally taken 25 community members through a six-month leadership development training program. At the end of the six months, he starts again with another 25. In this way he is building leadership in that community.

The strategy of Community Church of Joy was discussed in Chapter 2. Those who complete the four bases are admitted to the "Circle of Eagles." This group is the leadership of Community Church of Joy, and from this pool are drawn the persons who serve in leadership positions.

FIRST STEPS FOR LEADERS

Great Leaders Replace "To Do" Lists with "To Create" Lists

The implementation of Total Quality Ministry starts with the leadership. After the leadership has internalized the benefits of Total Quality Ministry, the next question is "Where do we begin?"

Just as in Chapter 4, where the implementation of a new program began with plans, the initiation of Total Quality Ministry starts with plans. To assist leaders, many businesses establish a "Quality Leader" or "Quality Team." While the Quality Team may be part of the leadership body or may include others, it must have direct and available access to the senior staff person, the senior/solo pastor. If a single individual is selected as the Quality Leader, the same access is necessary. The leader or team may be staff, volunteers, or a combination.

The Quality Leader/Team has the responsibility to oversee the Quality program. The leader/team will be the "quality conscience" for the congregation. This leader/team will be the resource for process improvement discussions and will facilitate problem solving and decision-making meetings. The leader/team will assist in interpreting the long range strategic planning and quality goals into annual action plans. This leader/team will assist in gaining the statistical thinking attitudes among the staff and volunteers. The selection of this leader/team is very important to the success of the process.

The first step for the leader/team will be their training in Total Quality Ministry. Next, it is likely that the leader/team will require specific training in facilitating decision making, problem solving, and other quality processes. Frequently, businesses will contract training from consultants until a person within the business has been fully trained and given the responsibility to be the trainer for that business. Given the widespread implementation of Total Quality Management, it is possible that congregations may already have persons trained in TQM. With some additional

training and guidance in Total Quality Ministry to recognize the differences
in the two programs, that person may be able to take the responsibility of
congregational trainer.

Plan the Quality Plan

When the leader/team understands the quality processes, it is in a
much better position to implement the quality plans. As with the other
strategic plans, the leader/team chooses a 3-, 5-, or 10-year look at quality
to determine where the congregation needs to be with respect to quality at
the end of that time. These long-term objectives may be quite general and
represent basic ideals. Based on these objectives, shorter-term goals are
established, which are then followed by annual policies and action plans.
All these quality goals, plans, and policies will become part of the overall
congregational strategic plan. Each time the strategic plan is reviewed or
generates policies, the quality goals and policies are also brought forward.

The Quality Leader/Team will address all aspects of Total Quality Ministry—from employee involvement to customer identification, from
training plans to resource needs for quality implementation, from staffing
needs for quality to employee recognition and award systems. An organization does not suddenly wake up one morning to say "Today we are a Total
Quality Ministry." Areas of implementation of the principles of Total Quality Ministry are planned in advance. One of the greatest challenges will be
fostering employee involvement (see Chapter 7). People do not naturally
embrace change. Many times they need to be convinced of the benefits.
The leader/team might pick a particular program or service to demonstrate
how this new process will be of benefit to all. Seeing success in one program, participants will be more willing to accept change in other areas.

It may be part of the leader/team's responsibility to conduct quality
assessments. An assessment checks the status of the quality program at a
particular time. It seeks to measure the level of customer satisfaction, the
level of employee involvement, the progress in reducing deficiencies, and
other aspects of the quality processes. The results of the assessment will
also provide valuable input to those areas that may require the greatest
attention. Sample assessment questions have been listed under "Practical
Application" in Chapters 2-9. Consider each set of questions and gauge
where your congregation's strengths and weaknesses lie with respect to
quality. Self-assessments and assessments from outside organizations can
both be of value to the congregation.

The Quality Leader/Team's work is not complete with the development of plans or design of the program. Total Quality Ministry is a process, not an endpoint. The leader/team continues to meet regularly to assess progress toward quality goals. It helps to evaluate the data collected throughout the quality process (see Chapter 6), and doing so assists in encouraging continuous improvement.

CORPORATE CITIZEN

As we discuss leadership, it should be said that effective congregational leadership also has an impact on the community. Through the ministry programs provided and the mission accomplished, the community is made aware of the congregation. The congregation then can become influential in that community. It may be influential in establishing the morals, values, and ethics of that community.

In Phoenix, the pastors of more than 30 African-American congregations have united to focus their efforts on children. Tired of the drive-by shootings, the drug dealing, the gangs that they say are strangling communities and destroying their youth, they have committed to work through the obstacles to make change happen.

Churches Uniting in Global Mission (CUGM) is an organization involving Christian congregations of all denominations. They have established the "Peace Maker Awards" program to help in creating caring communities. It is an encouragement for action to change the world for children who are victims of gang violence, crime, and abuse.

When the congregation views the community as a customer, what services will be provided to this customer? How may the quality of these services be improved? As congregational leaders seriously consider this customer and its needs, it will begin to serve as a corporate citizen.

Mainline churches have recently been described as "old-line" or "sideline" churches. The mainline churches can make a difference in their communities.

Total Quality Ministry Can Bring "Mainline" Churches
Back to the "Main Line"

CONGREGATIONAL SELF-ASSESSMENT

Is the congregational leadership fully supportive of quality ministry to the point of committing the necessary resources (financial, human, and so on) to its implementation? Is the congregational leadership ready to make decisions in favor of Total Quality Ministry? Is the congregational leadership ready to place the needs of the customer ahead of the organization's needs? Use this continuum to rate your congregational leadership.

```
├────┼────┼────┼────┼────┼────┼────┼────┼────┤
1    2    3    4    5    6    7    8    9    10
```

| Not Involved | Somewhat Committed in Certain Areas | Excellent Commitment to Quality Improvement in All Areas |

Has the senior/solo pastor implemented Total Quality Ministry in all areas of ministry? Are the individual ministry leaders using the tools and techniques of Total Quality Ministry based on the direction and leadership of the senior/solo pastor? Are quality topics part of the strategic planning and annual planning efforts? Are the staff and volunteer groups being trained in Total Quality Ministry?

```
├────┼────┼────┼────┼────┼────┼────┼────┼────┤
1    2    3    4    5    6    7    8    9    10
```

| Not Involved | Implementation in Some Areas/to Some Degree | Fully Implemented in All Areas, All Staff & Volunteers Trained |

© *Total Quality Ministry: Congregational Self-Assessment*, The JOY Company, 1994

PRACTICAL APPLICATION

With your leadership team, answer the following questions.

1. Who are the true leaders of your congregation, and how well do they support quality improvement and its attendant costs?
2. How does or should the leadership communicate the importance of quality improvement to others in the organization?
3. What is or should be the senior/solo pastor's current role in leadership and in management in establishing quality?

4.   How is your ministry providing a positive effect on the community?

Quick Responsiveness to Needs, Unity of Purpose, Anticipation and Expectation, and Leadership Development are the **QUAL** in Quality. The next chapter focuses on the **I** in Quality.

Chapter 6

Q
U
A
L
I nvestigating Results
T
Y

First Church continued to grow in membership. However, the worship attendance stayed the same. Every year the membership classes seemed successful, yet there was really no significant change in involvement.

The pastor and leaders wanted to know how the congregation could do a better job. One leader suggested a careful investigation. They discovered that they had a serious communication problem with the new members. It took six months to get a new member into the computer system, so regular church mailings were not getting to new members during their first six months of membership.

The information process had a serious gap. Six months was much too long. Lyle Schaller warns that after three months, many of the new members will lose interest unless an intentional process of assimilation has been implemented. Investigating results is essential for a church to carry out a quality ministry.

Actual measurement is essential. Not only knowing what to measure, but measuring the right way is important. The story is told of Pastor Bob who, feeling very ill, was also quite disoriented. Instead of using a thermometer to check his temperature, he used a barometer. He was found to be dry and windy.

THE NEED FOR MEASUREMENT

Total Quality Ministry emphasizes the necessity to provide measurable data for evaluation. We all have our impressions and feelings about how we are performing and how the ministry is going, but measurable statistics present the information in a manner that eliminates guesswork.

The Numbers Are Not the Goals

Once goals are set, measurable quantities are established to check progress toward those goals. Membership growth numbers should not be the goal of the congregation. Rather, the goal may be the creation of an environment and development of an effective quality process that lead to growth. The membership numbers are then important to determine progress toward that goal.

If the electrical power was lost to the scoreboard in the last few minutes of a basketball game, we all would continue to enjoy the play of the game, but soon there would be disagreements over who was leading and what was the score. Each spectator would have his or her impression, but the truth could be quite different. Soon the crowd would erupt in frustration.

The same is true in ministry. While one staff person may evaluate the performance in one way, others see the same ministry service in a different light and might evaluate the performance completely differently. Although both may be correct in their own thinking, the evaluation has not resulted in improving the quality of the service.

As Community Church of Joy began the implementation of statistical measurement, we encountered staff reluctance when we asked each ministry leader to keep statistics on involvement in that ministry. This reluctance was not anticipated and was the result of fear. The fear was that the results might show areas of weakness of the employee, or that more work was necessary in an area of ministry when the employee was already working very hard, or simply that the results might be misunderstood.

J. Edwards Deming, often referred to as the "Father" of quality management, places on management the responsibility of driving out fear. The staff training should address this factor and assure staff that the purpose of Total Quality Ministry is to improve the processes. While additional work may be required initially, the processes will become more efficient and more productive. If the 80/20 rule applies to time management, then 20 percent of the work requires 80 percent of the time available. Total Quality

Ministry focuses on efficiency and hates waste. Ministers should be ministering, and quality ministry gives them the time to do that.

STATISTICAL THINKING

Measurable data is essential for the evaluation and improvement of quality. Leaders need to be able to read and interpret statistical information. Training may be required for some congregational leaders who will be making decisions based on the collected data.

We Need to Understand before We Can Be Understood and We Need to Listen before We Can Be Heard

Statistical thinking promotes decisions based on fact and data rather than opinions. Statistical thinking understands that there is always "data scatter" or normal variation in measurable data. This variation may be due to measurement error or a variety of contributing factors. The statistical thinker knows better than to take corrective actions on normal variations.

Statistical analysis allows us to interpret historical data and trends to determine appropriate improvements and predict expected outcomes.

At Community Church of Joy we were surprised at a very low attendance figure at one particular service only to find that the person taking the count estimated the attendance, whereas the usual counter actually counted heads. The single low count was of concern, but since it was out of the norm, no specific actions were planned until further information was gathered.

Worship service attendance is a good example of data that fluctuates regularly. Individuals have attendance patterns that may be difficult to predict on an individual basis but become easier to predict in larger samples. The attendance on any Sunday can be greatly influenced by the weather, sporting events, vacations, special speakers, and so forth. When you average attendance figures to "smooth out" the specific variations, it becomes possible to see meaningful trends.

SELECTION OF DATA TO MEASURE

A significant amount of energy can be expended collecting and analyzing data, only to find that the data is not really measuring what you need to know. Counting the cars in the parking lot during worship may not make sense if the parking lot is only half full and the question is whether there is excess parking. It may make sense if you are measuring the average number of attenders per car or if you are measuring the changing number of cars over a period of time.

The selection of data to be gathered depends on the specific process being measured. Quality by design requires that before a service or ministry is started, the mission is defined, and goals and objectives are written— along with the identification of measurable data to determine the effectiveness of the service and the customer satisfaction. The objective determines the measurement tool. A head count of persons attending adult education classes in a week is a piece of data that has meaning but may not accurately indicate the number of individuals attending adult education classes. Some may be attending more than once. Design the measurement tool to meet the specific objective to be measured.

Measurements used by product manufacturers may be easier to define than those used by the church or other service providers. Attempt to use terms and units that are customary in the service industry. Measurements such as timeliness measured in days, minutes, and so on, or courtesy measured on a scale of highly satisfied to highly dissatisfied, are common. At times a new measurement tool will be developed to fit the particular need.

At Community Church of Joy, we have been calculating the membership numbers as a measure of the growth of the ministry. We have measured the attendance figures as a parallel effort. The first number tells us about the commitment level, and the other number helps us to identify the number of visitors attending each week. Our thought is that the visitors become the pool of potential new members.

In recent years, however, we have noticed that many of the persons in the prospect pool remain in the pool, and although they may attend regularly, they are not interested in making the commitment to membership. Several other churches have noticed this trend as well. These "serial participants" may associate with several churches and shop among churches based on their feelings at the time. Some participate with the youth program at one church while associating with the children's program at another and attending a mid-week service at still another.

While we continue to track membership numbers, we keep in mind that they do not indicate all those persons touched by the ministry. Weekly attendance figures do not accurately measure influence either, since many will be visitors. We do have a responsibility to encourage the growth of those who are not members but are regular attenders. Therefore, we are developing a new statistic to measure—*involvement*.

Involvement seeks to measure those individuals who are affected by the ministry enough to be involved in some way. We are seeking to develop a specific, statistically measurable value that can be used consistently to make comparisons and evaluate needs for improvement.

USING THE RIGHT MEASUREMENT TOOLS

Just as a barometer cannot be used for measuring temperature, a thermometer calibrated in degrees Celsius will not provide direct indication of degrees Fahrenheit. We must select the right measurement tools so that our measurements are correct.

It is essential that we measure the right things and that we measure them correctly. A surgeon would not think of performing surgery without first having the right diagnosis, the right tools, and the right procedure. Like gauging temperature or performing surgery, all the correct measurement tools must be in place before ministry can be evaluated.

We may desire to know the number of people involved in prayer ministry. It may have 1000 people in attendance at prayer events each month, but it may truly be 250 people each attending four events. Both are true measurements, but which actually measures the parameters desired?

The data to be collected must be consistently available. It will serve no purpose to develop a measuring device and change that device. Data collection must be consistent, reliable, and as free from outside influences as possible.

In Arizona, cultural factors are revealed in the large numbers of persons arriving at worship several minutes after the start of the service. Frequently, people will be from 5 to 10 minutes late. If the attendance count is taken immediately on some Sundays and later in the service on others, the method of measurement introduces errors. Data to be taken should be consistent at each measurement cycle. Juran states that the ideal unit of measure

1. is understandable in that it uses standardized terms.
2. provides an agreed upon basis for decision making.
3. applies broadly such that others may also be using the unit.
4. is conducive to uniform interpretation.
5. is economic to apply so that the cost of measuring the data is reasonable.
6. is compatible with existing designs of measurement instruments.[1]

It will almost always be necessary to rely on people to take the measurements. At these times it is helpful to understand that there are errors inherent with human measurements. People are subject to misinterpretation of what data is desired, or they may not understand the accuracy requirements of the data requested. While some processes may find estimates to be sufficient, others may require more exact measurements. Some people may not understand the terms or may interpret the terms in a different manner from that intended. Some people may not have the aptitude, training, or education required for the specific measurement. Anyone taking even the simplest measurements must be trained and should have written guidelines to follow. If the data is important enough to measure, it is important enough to measure correctly.

People may distort the data taken because they are predisposed toward a particular outcome or fear one of the possible outcomes. This distortion may be a conscious or subconscious error. At times people may distort data because they fear blame by a supervisor for an "incorrect" response. Distortions may occur as people minimize improvement so that another "improvement" may be recorded the next time. It is necessary to implement methods to attempt to "error-proof" the measurement. One method may be to establish the measurement in such a way that the person does not understand how his or her error will influence the outcome.

EXAMPLES OF DATA COLLECTED

Data collected at Community Church of Joy covers a wide range of statistics. While these examples are useful for this congregation, each congregation will need to choose its own areas to monitor based on its own mission, strategy, and policies. The following list is not exhaustive of required record keeping, but it serves as an example of data to be collected for analysis.

1. Membership: baptized, confirmed, and households.
2. Worship attendance: at each service, the total people present, number of members/guests, comparisons of attendance at each of the five weekend services, comparisons of guest attendance at each service.
3. Member attendance percentages for weekend services.
4. Total offerings: specific, general, and capital fund.
5. Attendance at ministry events, small groups, and classes: adult, youth, children, prayer, singles, seniors, and so on.
6. Commitment card pledges.

7. Contribution records.
8. Age profiles.

MEASUREMENT OF DEFICIENCIES

The cost of failures in the service provided can be very high, but frequently the cost is not known. The member who is unintentionally
slighted by a breakdown in service may quietly disappear and never return.
This may be discovered at some point when someone notices the absence,
but frequently the loss is simply accepted as a personal choice by the individual. Many churches fail to measure and learn from their ministry service
deficiencies.

If a person does register a complaint, the complaint is rarely given to
the person who has the ability to correct the deficiency. Frequently, these
complaints are simply forgotten and rarely are transmitted further. In addition, less than 5 percent of dissatisfied customers actually make formal
complaints.

The Church Membership Initiative project was undertaken in
Lutheran congregations to understand and address the decline in baptized
membership. While the results of the project were very revealing, one of
the features was the selection of focus groups to study former Lutherans'
attitudes about Lutheran congregations. Without attempting to evaluate
statistical information through the focus groups, four significant responses
were noted.

1. Former Lutherans (currently churched or unchurched) left because
   they felt the Lutheran congregation failed them in their time of greatest need (i.e., divorce, personal crisis, loss of job, emotional
   difficulties, problems with children, and so forth).

2. Former Lutherans who were now members of other denominations
   retained some level of hostility concerning the negative experience
   that caused them to leave the Lutheran congregation.

3. The former Lutherans who were not members of any congregation
   politely answered questions about what might increase their interest in
   rejoining a congregation. However, their body language and voice tone
   strongly suggested that they were simply politely answering questions.
   They showed no motivation to return.

4. The former Lutherans did not seem inclined to give Lutheran congregations another chance.[2]

This information is very sobering, and while it is likely that all denominations have these service deficiencies, we largely ignore or do not take the time to analyze the deficiencies enough to take measurable data. While manufacturing companies can measure number of defects per thousand or mean time between failures, service providers are left with the difficulty of assigning units of deficiencies.

In the design of services, measurement tools should be developed to detect these types of failures so that rapid feedback and response may be made. Nevertheless, all instances of ministry deficiency should be reported, measured, and analyzed so that the quality improvement of zero defects may be applied. There may be an opportunity to restore the individual before impassable walls are built.

Opportunities should be provided for your customers to provide feedback on the deficiencies in your services. Suggestion boxes, pew comment cards, confidential memoranda to the pastor, class comment cards, and many other methods are available to provide this feedback. These methods also help to reveal customer satisfaction or impressions. These opportunities must be immediately available at the time of dissatisfaction. If the customer must wait or search for a way to comment, you will never receive it. Making it easier to provide a complaint should increase the percentage of those who will complain and result in a truer measure of deficiencies.

Providing the comment forms will also demonstrate to the customer that you are willing to accept criticism, and this can increase the level of trust.

Exit interviews with those who leave your ministry can also point out deficiencies. A transfer of membership to another congregation as part of a move may be an accepted loss, but you may still gain valuable suggestions for improvement in an exit interview.

Measurement of deficiencies may take the form of simple counts of deficiencies, or it may be expressed in terms of a percentage, as a deficiency or error percentage. Such a measure may be determined by:

$$\text{Deficiency Percent} = \frac{\text{number of deficiencies}}{\text{number of opportunities for deficiencies}}$$

In business, deficiencies may result from the use of products in a manner for which they were not designed. Copy machines at Community Church of Joy have been found to frequently need service, hence that brand of copier gets a bad reputation. The evaluation determines that the need for service is because the copier is being used well beyond its designed capacity.

At times the correction of deficiencies may require a change in the perception of the customer. We have parking lot problems with pedestrians because they simply prefer to walk in the paved area rather than on the sidewalk, which is 5 feet away. A close evaluation of the information may uncover the perception, which will then lead to a solution.

At times deficiencies occur because a change in the service or ministry occurs, and the effect of that change is not evaluated in advance. The sound system designed for our sanctuary in 1982 was quite adequate for our needs at that time. Our worship styles have changed, and our needs have changed with them. Accordingly, our sound system can no longer deliver the quality of sound needed.

Some deficiencies occur because people may not be trained in the use of appropriate tools for avoiding the deficiency. A clear example is spelling errors in publications. Most word processors have a spell checker available, and one needs to know how to use it and use it consistently.

EVALUATION OF DATA

Quality Bases Decisions on Diagnosis, Not Preferences, Prescribed Programs, nor Previous Practices

Having data will be useless unless it is evaluated. An improper evaluation may be worse than no evaluation. The evaluation and interpretation of statistical data again requires the application of statistical thinking. How to evaluate the data is critically important. The evaluation of statistics has been compared to a Christmas present. The contents of the package is more important than the wrapping.

Graphing of collected data is frequently a direct, visual way of evaluating data and determining trends. Most congregations have persons with the ability to understand and use statistics to create meaningful charts and graphs. Find the person who understands what data needs to be measured, can translate this into data collection techniques, and is able to present this data in usable form. The graph on page 87 provides an example—in this case, average weekly attendance figures for 1992 and 1993 at Community Church of Joy. The graph isn't fancy and is easily generated by

computer or by hand. Once the data is presented, verify that it truly represents what you want to know, and then plan from it.

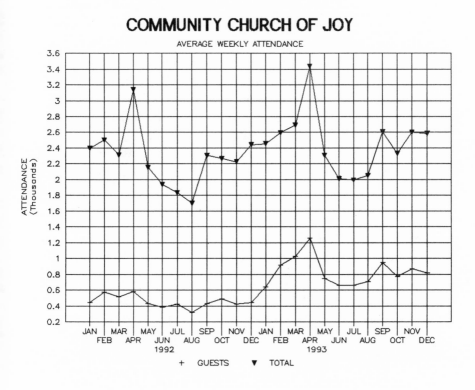

COMMUNITY CHURCH OF JOY
AVERAGE WEEKLY ATTENDANCE

One topic in the subject of algebra is the discussion of functions.
Functions allow the comparison of seemingly dissimilar quantities. Offerings
measured in dollars are not seemingly related to attendance measured in
terms of numbers of people. However, those who are involved in congregational statistics understand that there can be a direct correlation between
the number of people in church and the size of the offering. Understanding
the concept of the function, a person can seek to understand the relationship between various factors, and when understood, attempt to influence
the relationship in a positive direction.

Always Ask "Why" Five Times

An interview and tour with the Ritz-Carlton corporation (previous
winner of the Malcolm Baldrige National Quality Award) provided

valuable insight to quality programming. They have a strategy of five whys in investigating deficiencies. When a deficiency occurs, they ask the question "Why did that happen?" But they don't stop at the answer to that first "why." The first why may simply be a symptom to a deeper problem. They ask the question again, "But why did that happen?" The second, third, fourth, and fifth why usually get to the root of the problem. Seeing and understanding the root of the problem allows for the correction of the problem instead of the correction of one symptom.

Many people fear the evaluation of data. They fear the failures or deficiencies data might reveal. They might be the same people who fear the doctor's visit, believing it is better not to know the diagnosis. Total Quality Ministry welcomes the evaluation as an opportunity to improve. Knowing the diagnosis provides the information necessary to effect the cure.

Having Deficiencies Is Not Failure, But Not Correcting Those Deficiencies Leads to Failure

Seek to know the truth. Don't hide the bad news. Create an environment where data is shared, whether pleasant or unpleasant. Don't shoot the messenger of bad news. This may be obvious, but the culture of an organization can promote hiding bad news, even when leadership says it wants to know. Turn your negative news and data into opportunities for improvement. That "bad news" becomes a starting point for the improvement.

Realize that even your best shot may miss the target. But then ask, "How close did I come?" The apostle Paul said, "Not that I have already obtained this or have already reached the goal; but I press on to make it my own, because Christ Jesus has made me his own . . . forgetting what lies behind and straining forward to what lies ahead, I press on toward the goal for the prize of the heavenly call of God in Christ Jesus" (Philippians 3:12-14). Paul forgets what is behind. We do not hold on to our imperfections or failures, nor dwell on them, but use them as our starting point as we press on.

As congregational leaders, we think analytically, but also respond with grace. Seeking not to be judgmental in our evaluation provides a quality distinction for ministry—the *grace factor*.

The "Grace Factor" Is An Essential Factor

EXAMPLES OF DATA EVALUATION

As before, the data to be evaluated depends specifically on the quality goals, plans, and policies. The following provide examples of the data evaluated at Community Church of Joy. As before, this list is not exhaustive, but representative of types of evaluation.

1. Attendance trends—weekly attendance at worship is averaged for the month, and monthly averages are graphed to determine trends. This is accomplished for each service, comparisons among the five services, guest attendance, and member attendance.
2. Offerings trends—weekly offerings are averaged for the month and compared on a monthly and annual basis for trends.
3. Age profiles—profiles of previous years are compared with the current year to determine the changing demographics of the membership.
4. Top 50/100 givers—contribution records of the top givers are compared to previous years to predict trends in growth of member/ guest giving.
5. Attendance vs. offering—figures are correlated to determine the average gift per attender. This is analyzed for trends over a several- year period.
6. Membership losses—the list of all deletions from the membership rolls is provided to the pastor of pastoral care for follow-up.
7. The demographics—cross-section of members, including the number of single women, single men, married women whose husbands are not members, and so on.

At times the data to be evaluated is created for a specific purpose, and when the purpose is served, the data is no longer collected. Be sure that if data is collected, someone will be using it for evaluation.

PREDICTIONS

The proper evaluation of data provides a wealth of information to be used in predicting future outcomes. It can be used for anticipating results and planning for them. Having a good measure of expectation is important when actually measuring the results. Are the results expected or anticipated? Why or why not? Again, this is a diagnostic tool for quality improvement.

When asked the secret of his success in hockey, Wayne Gretzky said that most players go to where the puck is. He goes to where the puck will be.

Using the data for predicting future trends allows us to anticipate problems and plan solutions before the problems arrive. This leads to quality improvement.

BENCHMARKS

As mentioned previously, teaching congregations can provide benchmarks that are useful in another congregation. Community Church of Joy encourages its staff to visit other churches and report on what is seen and experienced. This data provides information and suggestions for quality improvement. Staff visits may be announced in advance, or one may merely drop in for worship services. As a matter of courtesy, appointments must be made if staff time is requested. Every church should be available on Sunday for evaluation. If you are the one being visited, seek formal feedback so you can learn from the visit too.

CONGREGATIONAL SELF-ASSESSMENT

Does this congregation use measurable statistics in its decision processes? Are decisions based on data rather than emotion, conjecture, or tradition? Do the senior/solo pastor and ministry leaders understand the basics of graphing and interpretation of data? Use this continuum to rate your congregation.

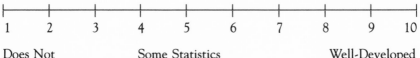

1	2	3	4	5	6	7	8	9	10

Does Not Use Statistics	Some Statistics for Some Activities	Well-Developed Statistical Thinking Processes

Does this congregation promote an atmosphere of openness concerning assessment information? Is it okay to find problems? Are the staff and volunteers encouraged to discover services and programs that do not work or that may show decline, or is there fear of being the bearer of bad news?

1	2	3	4	5	6	7	8	9	10

"Shoot the Messenger"	Some Fear but Discovery Is Okay	Atmosphere Supports Discovery and Correction

© *Total Quality Ministry: Congregational Self-Assessment*, The JOY Company, 1994

PRACTICAL APPLICATION

With your leadership team, evaluate the following items.

1. Are you collecting relevant, consistent data that is used in strategic planning, evaluation of performance, and measurement of customer satisfaction?

2. Are the leaders of the congregation able to think statistically? What special training are you doing?

3. How have you encouraged your ministry leaders specifically to collect benchmark data?

4. How does the congregation seek feedback from customers? Is it easy for the customer to provide it?

5. Does the congregation monitor deficiencies and probe to the depth and root of the deficiency?
6. How does the leadership create a climate and culture where bad news is received without judgment against the bearer?

Quick Responsiveness to Needs, Unity of Purpose, Anticipation and Expectation, Leadership Development, and Investigating results are the QUALI in Quality. The next chapter focuses on the T in Quality.

Chapter 7

Q
U
A
L
I
T raining, Education, and Development
Y

Pastor Benjamin decided to take one of his congregational members with him every time he made a hospital call or a home visit. This was an excellent training and development plan.

Soon after he began this process, he took his council president along on a hospital call. When they entered the patient's room, they began talking about the illness. Suddenly, the president blurted out, "I once knew a guy who died from your illness." The silence that followed was blaring.

Ben learned up close how important the training and development process was. In his eagerness to be a mentor, he skipped an important training step. Quality ministries are constantly training, educating, and developing people.

An organization's most valuable resources are its staff and volunteers. The organization will not have a quality ministry without the involvement and support of workers who are committed to the quality of the organization and see their individual part in contributing to that quality. We may refer to these persons as internal customers. We may also define internal customers as those who are involved in the operations of the congregation and who are also affected by its ministry. At times congregational members may be internal customers as they contribute to the ministry, and at other times they may be external customers as they partake of the ministry. This chapter focuses on those persons who are actively involved in making ministry happen in the congregation.

BUILDING A CHAMPIONSHIP TEAM

Lyle Schaller has said that either a church is staffed to grow or it is staffed to decline. Some of the most important decisions in the church concern who and when to hire. A good staff person enhances ministry, while a poor staff person diminishes ministry. An employee who does not understand or enthusiastically support your mission, vision, and strategy will do great harm when dealing with your customers. It is not likely that your external customers will be excited about your ministry if your employees are not.

The cost of releasing employees is very high—not only in the cost of training the replacement, but also in the cost of time in counseling, resulting from problems created by the departing employee. The whole process also saps energy, creates confusion, increases the work for others, and sets up opposing divisions among staff, leadership, and congregation. The cost of releasing employees may also include the cost of litigation.

It is therefore important to hire correctly.

Strategic planning was discussed in Chapter 3. Part of that planning should include the major staff positions. The plan should be detailed enough to set the priorities and order in which the major positions are filled. Support staff should be added when necessary. The first step in staffing is to follow the plan set in the strategic plan.

Many congregations are limited financially in the addition and development of staff. Volunteers may then fill the roles of the major staff positions until finances allow the hiring of those positions. Through the creation of unpaid staff positions, the positions indicated in the strategic plan may be filled even though funds do not exist for the salaries. Job descriptions that identify responsibilities and regular work hours, as well as other staff and human resource policies and procedures, apply to the unpaid positions. The unpaid staff members then become the professionals in planning ministry and its deployment. When funds become available, the unpaid persons may become paid employees. As with other staff positions, the unpaid staff persons are supervised by senior staff persons. Keeping all positions on a professional level creates greater commitment on the part of the unpaid person in his or her involvement with the ministry.

In Chapter 5, Leadership Development, it was reported that many congregations are finding greater ministry accomplished when the committee structure is reduced. Through the focusing of congregational energy in the *doing* of ministry rather than in committees deciding *how* ministry should be done, each volunteer finds greater fulfillment and joy. The staff members become the professionals entrusted to determine how ministry will be done and to develop the processes necessary to empower volunteers in accomplishing the ministry. In other words, the leadership decides on overall goals and objectives, and the various ministries are given responsibility for their accomplishment.

As the leadership determines the need for filling a position, a job description should be prepared. While all aspects of the job cannot be known before a person is hired, and the person certainly needs room for exercising his or her gifts, the job description should be detailed enough to check the "fit" with potential candidates. Leadership should have a good idea of what is expected in that position.

As you begin the search for the right candidate, pray for the calling of God to be placed in his or her heart. That call compels the person to seek the position and directs the candidate so that he or she cannot stay away. The advertising and search should present several qualified candidates.

Check references thoroughly, but also inquire concerning the person's feelings and attitudes toward your mission and vision. Areas that may seem to be only slight differences at the beginning have been known to grow to great chasms. Community Church of Joy also does psychological and personality testing as part of the application process.

Persons employed at Community Church of Joy must, in all but a few cases, be or become members. Since each is an ambassador and interfaces with the customer, each must be committed to the mission and vision of Joy. In addition, each person, again with a few exceptions, must also be committed to the five areas of maturing Christians noted in Chapter 4. As we highly value innovation and excellence in the services provided, we also seek those qualities in personnel. Finally, lead personnel need to be managers. As a staff-led church, the volunteers are involved in doing the ministry, so the staff must manage the volunteers and the programming.

MAINTAINING A CHAMPIONSHIP TEAM

Training generally refers to the encouragement and broadening of a specific skill and, as such, has a narrow focus. A word processing specialist may receive additional training in the latest revision of a word processing software program. Education implies a broader scope than training, as it relates to employee growth. Education may involve totally new areas for employees. Development provides the greatest breadth of growth. Through development, employees change skills and attitudes. Employees need to be trained in the techniques of total quality. Training should then lead to improvement in the way a job is done. Employees will also need education. New skills such as problem-solving techniques will be needed. Employees will need to develop a real understanding of the quality process. They will need to understand the reason for quality and their part in the process, internalizing the quality concepts so that they become important to them as individuals. Their attitudes will change.

A congregation cannot expect the team to remain a championship team unless it is continuously trained and developed. Certainly each member must keep up to date with the latest innovative techniques and programs. It is they who should be looking outside for potential benchmark programs. Using their specific gifts, new programs and services should be expected. They should be continuously challenged to look ahead, to be innovative, to risk, to strive for excellence, to develop breakthrough ideas.

> Breakthrough thinking comes not from continuing to look through our glasses at our work but from taking off our glasses and examining the lens.[1]

Are our lenses the right prescription for the 20/20 vision of today and tomorrow? With new "glasses" (new ways of viewing our environment), breakthrough ideas develop and incredible ministry results.

When asked about the cost of losing well-trained employees to other companies, Zig Ziglar responded, "There is one thing worse than training an employee and losing him. It is not training an employee and keeping him."

A person coming to a congregation's ministry needs to be educated and trained in the mission and vision in such a manner that it becomes her or his mission and vision. That may require more initial effort and time than learning the specifics of programming. If the staff person does not internalize the mission, it cannot be effectively spread to the unpaid staff, volunteers, and customers with whom he or she is in contact.

It has been said that people will forget the mission within a few weeks. That applies to staff as well. Regular training on various aspects of your mission and vision are necessary to keep all staff focused.

COLLABORATION

In discussing staff, Total Quality Management refers to the term *employee involvement*. This means that each employee not only does the job for which he or she was hired, but continuously seeks to improve the way he or she is doing the job. An involved employee doesn't simply perform a job. She or he is serving the customer. That customer may be an internal or external customer, but, nevertheless, the customer is being served.

The staff involved in Total Quality values the customers' needs and works to fulfill those needs every time in the best possible manner. Each person looks not only to their own needs but to the needs of others as well. This concept of employee involvement is not new to the Christian.

> If then there is any encouragement in Christ, any consolation from love, any sharing in the Spirit, any compassion and sympathy, make my joy complete: be of the same mind, having the same love, being in full accord and of one mind. Do nothing from selfish ambition or conceit, but in humility regard others as better than yourselves. Let each of you look not to your own interests, but to the interests of others. Philippians 2:1-4

This is more than people working together in cooperation. Collaboration among the staff means that each staff person not only does his or her job, but does it in such a way that it enhances the job others are doing. This is another meaning of employee involvement. All staff persons must understand that they are serving customers, and the quality with which they work is translated into the overall quality of the congregation. In this manner, each and every employee has the responsibility to use the gifts possessed to plan for quality, solve problems, and make improvements.

This step has been the most difficult for corporations truly committed to Total Quality. It takes a considerable effort to change the corporate culture. Most employees were hired to do a certain job, and as they become more and more proficient, it takes them less time, and they are able to handle more. It is a new idea that they should at the same time be thinking of improving the way they do their job or the way a product or process is designed.

The Seven Last Words of a Dying Church Are "We've Never Done It That Way Before"

This is also the common cry from employees trained in the old way of working. That way will not survive into the future.

Institutionalizing a culture based on continuous improvement requires a significant investment in time and resources. Employees must be trained to use new skills, given time to learn them, and encouraged to apply them on the job. Support and guidance must be provided throughout the process. On the average, 5% to 10% of people's time should be allocated for team activities, including training, meetings, and education. Eventually, the number of ideas generated and the percentage of these ideas implemented become important measures of both individual and team performance.[2]

It is important to point out that this effort will cost time and money. If each employee spends 10 percent less time doing the work currently assigned, someone needs to pick it up. The Ritz-Carlton organization requires 126 hours of training for each employee each year. Certainly, as each employee looks for ways to improve service, some inefficiencies will be eliminated. He or she may discover, however, that the service given the customer is not sufficient, and it requires more time. Time is required for the trainer to prepare, to train, and to monitor. Time is required for the follow-up. The initial training in the quality process may cost time and money.

Planning is required to prepare for implementation of Total Quality Ministry. Planning and allocating the finances in preparation for implementation can prevent surprises later. Some corporations did not adequately plan either the finances or the implementation and ran into trouble spending so much time on quality that the business itself suffered. The overall lesson learned from the corporate world, however, is that the benefits greatly outweigh the costs.

[Employee Involvement] has a number of advantages over traditional management systems:
- It replaces the adversarial "us versus them" mentality with trust, cooperation, and common goals.
- It helps develop individual capability by improving self-management and leadership skills, creating a sense of mission, and fostering trust.
- It increases employee morale and commitment.
- It fosters creativity and innovation, the source of competitive advantage.

- It helps people understand quality principles and instills these principles into the corporate culture.
- It allows employees to solve problems at the source immediately.
- It improves quality and productivity.
- It makes good business sense since two heads are better than one when it comes to identifying and solving problems.
- It is the dominant organizational model among world-class companies.[3]

Empowering the staff to make decisions and correct problems can require reorganizing the staff structure. It may even require restructuring the governing body's role. Many congregations are organized around committees. While a congregation may be experiencing success with the committee decision process, it is inherently slow and debilitating. The staff receives the opposite of empowerment by the fact that decisions are made elsewhere. A single good idea for improvement on the part of the staff may need to be approved through the committee, and by the time the approval is given, the opportunity may be lost. A congregation using this governing model should evaluate its effectiveness as part of the overall ministry quality improvement process. While committees and boards may be well suited for long-range planning of goals and objectives, they fall short at making them happen. The ministry should not exist to promote its organizational structure. The organizational structure both in staff and governance should exist to support the mission and ministry. It needs to be flexible enough to change when required.

Departments Create Compartments— Quality Builds Bridges Instead of Boxes

EMPLOYEE QUALITY IMPROVEMENT

Quality improvement with the individual employee is much like quality improvement for the congregation. Each employee must first identify all her or his customers, internal or external. For everything done, she or he must know who receives the benefit or the report, uses the data, or otherwise benefits from the effort. If no one does, maybe the effort is unnecessary. With that in mind, all employees must be able to identify their customers.

Next, the employee must identify the needs of the customers and plan how to best meet those needs. An employee truly interested in collaboration and quality will seek ways to improve the service to each customer. This leads to continuous improvement.

Just as the congregation may not know when deficiencies occur, employees may not know when their customers are less than satisfied with the product. Some employees will not provide criticism of another, even if it is constructive. When quality is internalized to the culture of the organization, each employee will seek out feedback.

The process may be made easier by developing a continuous feedback report. Internal customers respond to the supplier on a regular basis with customer satisfaction reports. Such reports are designed to be candid remarks concerning the products and services provided. While it is unlikely that the comments will truly be candid if the management is informed of the comments, these reports are between customer and supplier only. They may be verbal or written, but each employee is encouraged to provide such feedback.

Quality Fixes the Problems, Not the Blame

In many staff situations, an employee performs her or his responsibility and hands the product to another. At that time, it no longer is the first employee's responsibility. It belongs to another. When a problem occurs, each may point the finger at the person up or down the chain in handling the product or service. Total Quality Ministry means that each person in the chain owns the product or service. If a problem occurs, each person in the chain becomes a problem solver. The point is to fix the problem and not to point fingers.

Suppose that a customer arrives at church at night for a class and discovers that the scheduled room is closed, locked, and dark. After checking with those in other classrooms, she is still unable to find the room prepared for this class. As she inquires of others, she finally finds someone with a brochure that advertised the class and verifies her original room was correct. Finally, she sees someone who she believes to be a member of the maintenance staff and inquires why the room is locked. The staff person checks a list and replies that it is not on the list to open the room. By this time several other persons have gathered at the same location for the class. The staff person opens the room only to find that the room is not prepared for this class. In frustration, the class leader demands that the TV and

VCR be located and brought to the room. After 15 minutes the equipment is found and the class begins, but there is insufficient time to complete the session. All attenders are upset, the teacher threatens to quit teaching, and the maintenance staff person does not complete all the assigned work on time. His daughter has a band concert he cannot miss so he leaves, and in the morning a Bible study leader arrives to find that the TV and VCR that were in the classroom yesterday have suddenly disappeared.

The way this problem may have been solved in the past is to point the finger at the maintenance staff for not properly listing the class. They would then point the finger at the incorrect schedule they received. The scheduler would point the finger at the lateness of the input from the director. The director would note that the input was correct, but the bro-chure contained an error on the room number. The preparer of the brochure would complain that the copy was not properly checked.

While the root of the problem may not have been any of these events, the finger pointing has not resolved the problem but has aggravated it by damaging relationships among the staff, the volunteers, and the customers. Even if the problem was found, the process was not corrected in order to prevent a recurrence in the future.

Excuse Cushions Are for Spectators, Not for Participants

Total Quality Ministry places the responsibility for the final product on each person in the chain. All persons share the problem and therefore share in creating the solution. Fixing the problem becomes the joint task, not fixing the blame. Wherever the error or deficiency occurred, the whole team works on the solution. The result is overall process quality improvement.

Recently, department directors on the staff of Community Church of Joy complained of the red tape required to get something printed and mailed. While researching this complaint, others in the process also com-plained. While the director found the process cumbersome, the office assistant also was frustrated because she arranged the volunteers to do the mailing, and frequently the materials were not ready by the time the vol-unteers arrived. After all those affected provided their input, the process was diagrammed through the use of a process flow chart. That flow chart follows.

PROCESS FLOW CHART

Communications Design and Mailing

BEFORE

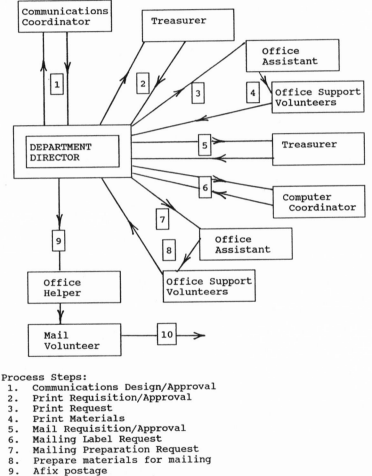

```
Process Steps:
 1.  Communications Design/Approval
 2.  Print Requisition/Approval
 3.  Print Request
 4.  Print Materials
 5.  Mail Requisition/Approval
 6.  Mailing Label Request
 7.  Mailing Preparation Request
 8.  Prepare materials for mailing
 9.  Afix postage
10.  Deliver to post office
```

Several unnecessary loops were found in the process, and it was these that made it cumbersome and contributed to the staff's frustration. A rework of the diagram developed a flow chart that eliminated all the loops and greatly streamlined the process. The revised chart follows.

PROCESS FLOW CHART

Communications Design and Mailing

AFTER

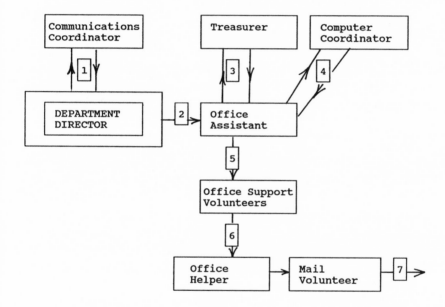

Process Steps:
1. Communications Design/Approval
2. Print and Mail Request
3. Funding Requisition/Approval
4. Mailing Label Request
5. Copy Materials and Prepare for Mailing
6. Afix postage
7. Deliver to Post Office

The directors found it easy to use; the office assistant could now properly plan resources and volunteers; and the required checks and balances were maintained.

Gone Are the Days When An Employee Can Say, "It's Not My Problem"

Any deficiency in the ministry is shared by the staff committed to the overall improvement of quality. Each deficiency becomes important to each staff person who then takes the responsibility to either correct the deficiency, gather the team necessary to do so, or formally deliver the deficiency to another. Dropping deficiencies through the cracks should never happen.

To expect employees to take this type of initiative requires that they be empowered to take action and make decisions. Guidelines need to be established so that employees know what authority they have in order to make the necessary corrections. As an example, employees should know what spending limits apply if the solution they arrive at will cost money.

STAFF EVALUATIONS

Assuming that rewards are given to encourage positive behavior, the purpose of a performance evaluation system is to provide information to the employee to improve positive performance.

Human relations departments teach us that performance evaluations are essential for the well-being of the employee and the organization. Frequently, salary actions are based on the results of the evaluation. Traditionally, the supervisor evaluates the performance of the employee, and the employee has the opportunity to respond. This type of evaluation turns into a time of judgment. The performance appraiser deals with strengths, which build self-esteem and pride, and weaknesses, which build shame. If the employee believes the supervisor is missing the mark, the evaluation itself may lead to poor performance.

The performance evaluation system for a staff that is implementing Total Quality Ministry is different. Since each person involved in a process is responsible for the quality, the team as a whole is evaluated. Internal and external customer satisfaction and product or service improvement must be included. The way a person responds to the team environment and his or her role in that team is important. Evaluations will become more subject to discussions of concepts such as teamwork, innovation, communication, cooperation, support, problem solving, enthusiasm, attitude, effort, and so forth.

The U.S. Navy of the 1970s required performance evaluations for each rate and rank to exactly match the bell curve. Five percent were exceptional; 20 percent were above average; 50 percent were average; 20 percent were below average; and five percent were unsatisfactory. If the numbers of persons in each category of each rate did not exactly match the percentages required, the evaluations were reworked until they did. The effect was very demoralizing for most involved. When one person's performance is compared with another's, it leads to problems. Instead, a person's performance should be compared to the goals, standards, and values of the mission of the organization and their own goals that contribute to the overall ministry.

Just as the evaluation contains input from internal and external customers and the supervisor, it should also contain input from the employee. The employee should be given the opportunity to conduct a self-evaluation. This evaluation is compared to that of the supervisor so that differences may be points of discussion. An employee conducting an honest appraisal will indicate his or her strengths and weaknesses. The evaluation then becomes a time of affirmation and encouragement.

RECOGNITION AND AWARDS

What Gets Rewarded Gets Done

Employees and volunteers like and deserve to be recognized for good work. Public recognition of excellent performance encourages that performance in the individual and in others who witness the praise. Congregations should seek ways to recognize employees and volunteers for outstanding work. The awards and recognition need not be costly in terms of money but should truly award excellence and quality.

While the authors were discussing this chapter over lunch, their comments were overheard by another person. The individual was a retired engineer from a major U.S. automobile manufacturer. He knew about continuous improvement quality and volunteered the following story.

The engineering department was committed to quality. The program for continuous improvement was emphasized. The engineers were encouraged to find new ways to improve each product. In fact, as part of the encouragement, a competition was developed between engineering teams. On the wall of the engineering department, each product was displayed as a horse in a horse race. For each product improvement made, the horse was moved along the track. The members of the team received the recognition and praise from the supervisor. The system was flawed, however, because the team that correctly engineered the product from the start required no product improvements, so the horse remained at the starting gate. The negative feedback received by this team led to engineered defects in the next product so that improvements could be made to move the horse to the finish line.

Misdirected awards are worse than no awards. If awards are to be given, make sure that the correct behavior is being rewarded.

Encourage recognition by internal customers. Provide opportunities for staff to publicly acknowledge outstanding performance by others. At the weekly staff meeting and prayer time at Community Church of Joy we have a regular feature called "Winners of the Week." We encourage staff persons to publicly recognize someone's work or effort that led to exceptional results during the previous week. It is usually a spirited time and is much appreciated by all. At several such times, one staff person's praise of another has led that person to praise someone who helped him or her. Such times help to foster collaboration and teamwork. The "winners" are also named in the staff notes circulated to all staff personnel and members of the board of directors. Written acknowledgements sent to staff members, with copies to management, may be another way to recognize exceptional performance. Such notes may be referred to during the performance review.

BENEFITS AND COMPENSATION

Many congregations are not proud of the compensation and benefits provided employees. Most ministries require high performance for low pay. They depend on the calling of the individual to keep them employed, for certainly few employees are paid what they might receive in the corporate world. For that reason, congregations should seek first to be fair with the compensation and benefits and then seek to provide additional benefits and perks where possible.

Annual compensation studies are available that provide compensation figures for all major categories of church staff and that are based on congregational size, denomination, budget, region, and so forth. Such studies are starting points in determining not what the corporate world might pay but what other comparable churches are paying. Such studies should be utilized by congregations in establishing salary ranges for each employee. Consistency and fairness in compensation is essential to maintain proper staff relations.

Total Quality Management also suggests that compensation should not be tied to performance reviews except for the exceptional performer. Salaries remain level within the salary range for all employees of that description except that the exceptional performers are placed higher in the range.

There is no question that the cost of benefits is high and continues to increase. Congregations should evaluate benefit programs to provide the greatest coverage to the greatest number of employees at the lowest cost.

EMPLOYEE SATISFACTION

Every employee desires a work environment that is safe, secure, and provides the environment where he or she can be creative. There are office spaces where storage boxes fill the hallways and are safety hazards. Hazards and clutter cannot lead to quality performance. Dark offices, poor phones, cramped quarters, and poor ventilation are all negative influences on employee production. Although funds may be tight, a small amount can go a long way in increasing employee satisfaction.

An issue that kept surfacing at Community Church of Joy was the accessibility of the office area after normal working hours. Some complained of the inconvenience of having to use the front door of the building when their office was located near the rear door. A team of four staff persons was formed to study the question. Their response was that it was more important to ensure the security of persons who were working late than to reduce the inconvenience. When placed in that light, security becomes more important.

Many corporations are also beginning to see the benefits to the company in being concerned for the overall well-being of the employee. Providing on-site child care, athletic activities, professional counseling, and interest groups are just a few examples. The same will apply to ministries that seek to care for the overall well-being of each employee.

CONGREGATIONAL SELF-ASSESSMENT

The greatest resource a congregation has for completing its mission is its people. These people are paid and unpaid staff and volunteers. In the overall management of this resource, evaluate the effectiveness of management. Does this congregation effectively place its volunteers in areas of their giftedness? Are the people empowered to do the ministry? Is the staff of paid and unpaid persons organized to support the volunteers in the service of ministry and programs? In the selection of staff, is the application and interview process well defined to select the right person for the position? Use this continuum to rate your congregation's management of volunteers.

1	2	3	4	5	6	7	8	9	10

No Overall Plan   Some Areas Are   Excellent Process of
for Volunteer and   Well-Planned/Others   Volunteer and Staff
Staff Effectiveness   Not   Placement and
                                                     Management

In this congregation are the paid and unpaid staff empowered with decision-making authority? Are volunteers in key leadership positions empowered to correct deficiencies? Does each staff and key volunteer understand his or her role in the overall quality of the ministry? Does each staff and volunteer treat others as highly valued customers? Do the staff and key volunteers collaborate in the work effort—considering how each may help the other in improvement? Is innovation and risk-taking (within limits) encouraged?

1	2	3	4	5	6	7	8	9	10

Decisions Made   Some Empowerment   Staff and Volunteers
by Selected Persons   of Selected Persons   Empowered, and
Only   Collaborate in
                                                     Excellent Manner

© *Total Quality Ministry: Congregational Self-Assessment*, The JOY Company, 1994

PRACTICAL APPLICATION

With your leadership team, evaluate the following concerns.

1. How are specific staffing needs addressed in your strategic plan?
2. Does your congregation provide funding and a specific structure for continuing education, training, and development? Which staff members are involved in this budget item?
3. How are you encouraging your employees to improve the quality of their output?
4. How have you created an environment where employees are empowered and encouraged to make improvement suggestions? Will their suggestions be honestly evaluated?
5. How does your compensation system ensure fairness to all employees? How does it specifically reward excellence and quality?
6. What opportunities do you (or should you) provide for public recognition and awards for excellence?
7. How do you provide opportunities for addressing the overall well-being of employees through recreational activities, counseling opportunities, day-care, safety, and security?

Quick Responsiveness to Needs, Unity of Purpose, Anticipation and Expectation, Leadership Development, Investigating Results, and Training, Education, and Development are the **QUALIT** in Quality. The next chapter focuses on the last principle in Quality, the **Y**.

Chapter 8

Q
U
A
L
I
T

Yield in Transformation of Lives

Sid was an ugly caterpillar with orange eyes. He spent his life groveling and squirming in the dirt on God's earth. One day Sid got a terrific idea. He crawled up the stem of a bush, made his way to a branch, and secreted a translucent fluid onto that branch. He made a kind of button out of the fluid, turned himself around, and attached his posterior anatomy to that button. Then he shaped himself into a "J," curled up, and proceeded to build a house around himself. There was a lot of activity for a while, but before long Sid was entirely covered up and you couldn't see him anymore.

Everything became very, very still. You might have concluded that nothing at all was happening. But, as a matter of fact, plenty was happening. Metamorphosis was taking place.

One day Sid began to raise the window shades of his house. He let you look in and see a variety of colors. On another day an eruption took place. Sid's house shook violently. That little cocoon jerked and shook until a large, beautiful wing protruded from one of the windows. Sid stretched it out in all its glory. He continued his work until another gorgeous wing emerged from a window on the other side of the house.

At this stage of Sid's life you might have wanted to help. But you didn't, for if you tried to pull the rest of Sid's house off, you would maim him for the rest of his life. So you let Sid convulse and wriggle his way to freedom without any outside intervention.

Eventually Sid got his house off his back, ventured out onto the branch, stretched, and spread his beautiful wings. He was nothing like the old worm he used to be. And do you know what? Sid didn't crawl back down the bush and start groveling and squirming in the dirt again. No indeed! Instead, he took off with a new kind of power—flight power. Now, instead of swallowing dust, Sid flies from flower to flower, enjoying the sweet nectar in God's wonderful creation.[1]

THE BOTTOM LINE

The books in the private sector concerning Total Quality Management not only state the importance of the quality process, but also predict failure for those companies that do not operate by such principles. The *yield* for the corporate world is stated in terms of improved customer relations, increased customer loyalty, increased market share, increased employee satisfaction, better products, reduced costs, greater word-of-mouth customers, and so forth, with an attendant increase in the net profits.

While the Bottom Line in Business Is Net Profit,
The Bottom Line in Total Quality Ministry
Is a Transformed Life

"Do not be conformed to this world, but be transformed by the renewing of your minds" (Romans 12:2a). The creator of quality is Jesus. Because of him, lives were and are transformed. The blind received sight, the lame walked, the sick were healed, the deaf heard, the dead were raised, dignity was restored, and salvation was assured.

The *third dimension* in Total Quality Ministry is that it seeks not only to identify the customers' needs and then meet the needs with quality, but also to transform their lives with the power of the gospel.

Understanding the customers and their needs allows the ministry to realize the barriers that people erect on their own path to a relationship with Christ. Understanding the barriers allows ministries to remove them where possible and to guide the people through those that cannot be removed.

Lyle Schaller said Community Church of Joy is a church that has a "low threshold" but "high risk" for people. By that he meant that Community Church of Joy has removed as many of the barriers as possible that stand between a person and Christ. The threshold to involvement at Community Church of Joy does not require a large or greatly noticeable step. However, there is great risk that once a person enters the life of this church, the person's life will be transformed forever.

The transformation that takes place results in lives that are changed. Those changed and transformed lives can be and will be seen by others. In Galatians, Paul describes the "fruit" of the spirit. Because of the Spirit's work, our outward behavior is no longer the same. In this sense, the transformation can be measured.

While each congregation must decide how to define and measure transformation, some descriptors of the transformation might be the following:

FROM	TO
Lukewarm	Committed
Passive	Active
Unemployed in the church	Called responsibility
Latent—undiscovered gifts	Gifted
Lonely—uncaring community	Supported—small group
Sidelined—no service	Placed to make a difference
Stable or declining	Growing, learning, practicing
Peripheral	Centered on Christ
Low expectations of church	Demanding high expectations
No fruit	Fruitful

Lyle Schaller often refers to several characteristics of transformed people who have been incorporated into the ministry. These characteristics follow.

1. Able to list at least seven new friends made in church.
2. Able to identify their spiritual gifts.
3. Involved in at least one role/task/ministry appropriate to their spiritual gifts.
4. Involved in a small group (or class).

5. Demonstrating a regular financial commitment to the church.
6. Personally identifies with the goals of the church.
7. Exhibiting a regular worship commitment to the church.
8. Excited about identifying unchurched friends and family members, inviting them to church, and helping them get involved.

A transformed person needs to be effectively and intentionally incorporated. Incorporation into the ministry may be measured in terms of regularity of worship service attendance, small group attendance, volunteer areas of service, regularity of financial support, participation in mission activities, teaching or attending adult education classes, and many other choices.

YIELD OF AN INCORPORATED, TRANSFORMED PERSON

The Bible is full of the imagery of yield. In the parable of the sower, Jesus talks of yield not in terms of 5- or 10-fold but in terms of 100, 60 or 30 fold. In today's world, two bushels of planted wheat will average a yield of 67 bushels; three bushels of planted oats will yield 79 bushels; and one-third bushel of corn will yield 120 bushels. Jesus is looking for a large harvest. He wants the greatest yield.

Churches are doing long-range planning as if the future is going to be an extension of the present. We are going to be surprised by change as we were so often in the past. . . . Christian organizations are tremendously slow. . . . What we need is a renaissance of Christian creativity applied to the emerging issues of tomorrow's world.

Indeed, in a decade when Christianity's position at the center of the religious stage is threatened, most churches are being "reactive" rather than "pro-active." The scholars among them read the present through the past. Combing case histories and tracing sociocultural change, they look backward for their understanding of current religious ferment.[2]

Just as the businesses of today need to adapt to the changing world of quality, so too do congregations. Congregations that will still be alive in the twenty-first century will not be in the preservation or conservation business but in the multiplication and transformation business. This is

much more than an issue of numbers of people, it is lives committed to
Christ.

EXCELLENCE IN MINISTRY

Total Quality Ministry moves us from doing what we have always done
to a passion for mission. As we first change our focus to see each person as
a customer, we seek to meet his or her needs each time. Then we seek to
continuously improve the service and ministry we provide. We seek to
exceed the customer's expectations and transcend beyond to amazement!
After all, isn't the gospel amazing?

Churches in decline may have a mentality of scarcity, of loss, of
destroyed crops. A commitment to quality can reverse the trend to yield a
bumper crop. As we try to substitute excuses for success, quality leads us to
accountability.

Many say that we are not called to be successful; we are called to be
faithful. Total Quality Ministry calls us to be effective while we are
faithful.

The Church Membership Initiative project was undertaken to understand and address the decline in the Lutheran congregations from 1970 to
1990. Its overall objective was, "To set in motion forces that will result in
annual increases in the number of members of Lutheran congregations."[3]

One general insight that captures the spirit of the findings from the
entire project is that, "Solutions are found within individual, motivated
congregations taken one at a time."[4]

While this report addresses the Lutheran congregations, the findings
probably fit all dominations. It is up to each congregation to examine its
own ministry, its own treatment of customers, its own quality or lack of
quality.

Total Quality Ministry unlocks congregational potential, which produces the best and strongest Christian church possible.

Life transformation is the yield. How that is measured is the responsibility of each congregation to determine. Jesus was not satisfied with 99
percent. He came so that *all* might be saved.

CONGREGATIONAL SELF-ASSESSMENT

Does this congregation consider life transformation as a key part of its mission? Has this congregation determined the meaning in measurable terms of a transformed life? How is a transformed life visible in this congregation and ministry? Use this continuum to rate your congregation's attitude toward life transformation.

```
|----+----+----+----+----+----+----+----+----|
1    2    3    4    5    6    7    8    9    10
```

Don't Know	Life Transformation Is Important, but Not Measured	Life Transformation Is an Essential, Measurable Part

For the key points and the data provided, evaluate this congregation for meeting its mission. What trends can be seen in the transformation of lives as a result of this ministry? Is this congregation effective in meeting its mission? Are lives being transformed as a result of this ministry? Use this continuum to rate your congregation's effectiveness in ministry.

```
|----+----+----+----+----+----+----+----+----|
1    2    3    4    5    6    7    8    9    10
```

No Measurement Taken	Average or Marginal Improvement	Positive Trends, Mission Is Being Accomplished

© *Total Quality Ministry: Congregational Self-Assessment*, The JOY Company, 1994

PRACTICAL APPLICATION

With your leadership team, consider the responses to the following:

1. Are you a growing, stagnant, or declining congregation at this time? Is life transformation an important part of your mission?
2. How are you improving the quality of your ministry? What should you be doing that you may not be doing now?
3. What is the yield of your ministry? How is it measured?

Quick Responsiveness to Needs, Unity of Purpose, Anticipation and Expectation, Leadership Development, Investigating Results, Training, Education, and Development, and Yield in Transformation of Lives spell **QUALITY** for Total Quality Ministry. Where do we go from here? Let's get started!

Chapter 9
Getting Started

The purpose of this book has been to identify the tremendous benefits to the Christian church in the implementation of Total Quality Ministry. It was not intended to be the final word on the subject. Now, the question that begs to be answered is "What would be the initial steps in the implementation of the Total Quality Ministry process?"

First we must note that all congregations are not alike in ministry, in organization, in governance, in size, in location, and so forth. Each congregation will proceed in implementation of Total Quality Ministry in an individualized manner. Nevertheless, the unifying principles in this book can be applied to each congregation, and certain implementation techniques will also apply. As you have completed the self-assessments and the discussion topics at the end of each chapter, you will undoubtedly have discovered areas in which you are doing well as well as areas that need improvement. Again each congregation will differ in the areas to which attention is needed.

Most congregations will find the general outline that follows to be helpful in getting started.

LEADERSHIP

Getting started begins with the leadership and management of the congregation. As noted in Chapter 5, "Leadership Development," the congregational leaders, including the senior/solo pastor, must be committed to the Total Quality Ministry process. Training of this leadership team in the basics of Total Quality Ministry will be required. The leadership team includes the primary permission givers in the congregation.

The commitment to the Total Quality Ministry process is necessary so that financial and human resources will be allocated for quality; decisions made throughout the process will be based on quality; organizational focus will be on the customer; the organizational structure of the congregation will be open discussion and review; major decisions on mission, vision, values, and strategic planning will be made; and the whole congregation will be educated in Total Quality Ministry. A solid commitment to the process will help you deal with the questions, comments, and concerns that will arise from congregational members.

MANAGEMENT COMMITMENT

The commitment of management is the next step. The management of the congregation is not necessarily the same as its leadership. Certainly the senior/solo pastor is a member of both, but the management team will be responsible for the daily implementation of Total Quality Ministry. Through the training of staff and volunteers, the balance of the management team will become committed to the process. This training is lead by the senior/solo pastor. This commitment cannot be delegated.

QUALITY ASSESSMENT

Following the completion of leadership training, the leadership and senior/solo pastor will conduct an assessment of the current level of quality in the ministry. The assessment is conducted at this point to provide information to the leadership and management concerning the starting point of the congregation. It will be a point of reference in later assessments. It is also done here as a tool to assist the Quality Leader/Team to carry out one of its functions noted below.

QUALITY LEADER/TEAM

Picking the Quality Leader or the Quality Team members is the next step. It is possible that this team not include any of the leadership of the congregation. The selection of this person or team should be based on abilities and gifts to fulfill the Quality Leader/Team role. As noted before, this person or team becomes the *quality conscience* for the congregational management team. If resources are available, this function may be filled by a staff quality leader. This person should report directly to the senior/solo pastor. If resources are not available, this team may consist of several volunteers. If this role is given as an additional duty to an existing staff person, the total expectations of that person's entire work activity must be considered.

QUALITY LEADER/TEAM TRAINING

The Quality Leader/Team then will be trained thoroughly in Total Quality Ministry concepts and practices. This person or team will be the congregation's in-house quality expert. This team will arrange and provide the quality training for the staff and volunteers; it will keep the quality focus of the staff and volunteers in their daily functions; it will assist the leadership and management teams in the planning of quality projects and annual improvement plans for quality; it will keep the congregation's focus on the customer; and it will facilitate staff and volunteer decision making and problem solving. It will perform the other functions as determined necessary by management and leadership to implement the Total Quality Ministry process.

PROJECT SELECTION

Quality improvement projects are a part of the larger effort to transform the organization. While the congregational management may wish to immediately start implementation of the principles in all aspects of the ministry, the overall transformation of the organization will take time. It will take time to plan effectively each project to be implemented. Many congregations may need to start at the very basic of questions, "What is our mission?"

The urge to immediately implement wholesale changes through Total Quality Ministry should be resisted in favor of planning and picking a specific area in which to start. With the proper planning and implementation, the selected project will be successful. A successful project will create greater enthusiasm on the part of the staff and volunteers and will demonstrate success to the management. With this success and experience in planning, more projects may be selected. In addition, the discipline of improving the first project's processes may be spread. This sets the example for the entire staff and volunteers.

Thus, management and leadership must select the first project.

Concurrent with the selection and training of the Quality Leader/ Team, the quality assessment is conducted. This tool will provide information on the current level of quality in each area of the principles of Total Quality. This will assist the Quality Leader/Team in determining the areas requiring greatest attention. From this information, one or two initial projects for improvement and implementation of the Total Quality Ministry principles will be recommended. The management team will then work with the Quality Leader/Team to complete the selection of the project and to implement the quality processes.

PROJECT ASSESSMENT

In the planning of the selected project, checkpoints throughout the project are determined, along with an assessment of the final service or program quality. This is used in the feedback to improve the process.

In like manner, new insights will be gained through the process of implementation of Total Quality Ministry in the selected project. The methods and techniques used to implement quality in the first project can then be improved upon and used when new projects are selected for quality improvement. Not only are projects and processes improved, but the way in which quality is implemented is also improved. Quality then becomes a way of life in this congregation.

At appropriate times, and perhaps annually, the overall quality of the ministry is evaluated. Using again the congregational self-assessment tool, congregations can determine where they are and how far they have progressed in Total Quality Ministry. In the final analysis, the bottom line for the congregation is lives transformed into living relationships with Jesus Christ through the power of the Holy Spirit!

CONGREGATIONAL QUALITY ASSESSMENTS

The Malcolm Baldrige National Quality Award is an annual award that recognizes U.S. companies that excel in quality management and quality achievement. The award promotes an awareness of quality as an increasingly important element in competitiveness, an understanding of the requirements for quality excellence, and the sharing of information on the benefits of successful quality strategies.

The JOY Company has taken the Malcolm Baldrige Award criteria and interpreted it for the Christian church. A ministry seeking excellence in its quality may wish to review the criteria for the Malcolm Baldrige award or The JOY Company interpretation and have its own operation evaluated with respect to this level of quality. The JOY Company has also developed a congregational self-assessment tool that may be helpful for a congregation to assess the quality of its ministry on its own.

The Malcolm Baldrige National Quality Award packets of award criteria or application forms and instructions may be ordered free of charge by calling (301) 975-2036 or writing:
Malcolm Baldrige National Quality Award
National Institute of Standards and Technology
Route 270 and Quince Orchard Road
Administration Building, Room A537
Gaithersburg, MD 20899-0001

The JOY Company interpretation of these criteria or the congregational self-assessment tool may be requested by writing:
The JOY Company
16635 N. 51st Avenue
Glendale, AZ 85306

PRACTICAL APPLICATION
With your leadership team, respond to the following questions.

1. Is this leadership team committed to Total Quality Ministry and the transformation it can lead to in this congregation?
2. Who will be our Quality Leader or members of the Quality Team?
3. Who is responsible for completing the congregational self-assessment, and when will it be completed?
4. When will we complete the training of the Quality Leader/Team?
5. Who will be the decision makers for the project selection for quality improvement?
6. What is our target date for the implementation of Total Quality Ministry in our congregation through this project?

Conclusion

Imagine the Dead Sea becoming a freshwater lake. The Dead Sea is smelly, salty, and stale. A freshwater lake is crisp, clean, and clear.

Transformation is when a dead sea becomes a freshwater lake.

The dead sea in ministry represents stale, stuffy, ineffective processes that choke out life and growth. The dead sea mentality is a result of fossilized structures and systems that create bureaucracy. Fossilization comes from being inflexible and unable to make quick adaptations to changes in the world in which we live. Rigidity comes from placing security in structure.

The people who resist change must have their security in methods, systems, structures, and styles. However, if our security is in Christ—if Christ is the stabilizer in our life—in the midst of an earthquake of change in methods, structures, systems, and styles, we can remain secure.

The truth is that old methods (successful as they may have been) do not work with new challenges. When the fresh water of new ideas flows, the dead sea force forms a union that seeks collective resistance. This dead sea power block becomes more vocal the more creative and innovative the idea becomes.

Total Quality values a continual process of innovation—anticipating people's needs before they even ask and effectively meeting those needs in ways that go beyond expectation. John Naisbitt, author of *Megatrends 2000*, has said "We all need to reinvent what we are up to. It's a matter of survival."

Survival was very important to the people of Transfiguration Lutheran Church in The Bronx, New York. When Pastor Heidi Neumark arrived 10 years ago, the church had 15 members and was about to die. The remaining leadership said their love for the church was stronger than the fear of change. So they developed a mission statement around their name Transfiguration. It included the vision to see beyond the present, and the transformation of lives through the power of God's love.

They studied the culture and context of their location. Located in the poorest congressional district in the nation, they have now grown to over 120 in the two worship services. One service is in English, the other Spanish. They minister to between 500 and 1000 people each week through support groups, after school, and other programs. Recently they started a building program. They are building where the parking lot is now located because their members don't own many cars.

Pastor Heidi Neumark remarked that Transfiguration Lutheran shared a lot in common with Community Church of Joy in that both studied the needs in their areas and responded to those needs. Both have a good understanding of mission and context.

The transformation must begin within. Structures, styles, methods, or systems don't change until people do. Attempting to change anything without changing ourselves is like trying to improve a golf game without developing the skills to make a better game possible.

Peter Lowe has interviewed and studied the success strategies of the top achievers of the world. In his "SUCCESS 1994" seminar, he said, "There is no success without transformation."

The Bible tells us to not be conformed but to be transformed by the renewing of our minds. This process is not simply improving the old, it is inventing the new!

Total Quality Ministry Isn't a Church Program, It's a Way of Programming the Church

Everyone who deeply loves the church cares about the Total Quality Ministry of the church. For too long the church has lost its quality focus. Because of that, the Christian church has suffered significant setbacks, membership loss, financial decline, negative public influence, and worst of all, indifference.

It is time for all of us who love the church to take a courageous stand for quality in ministry. Some of the telltale signs of slippage are sloppy worship services, poorly trained teachers, run-down buildings, weed infested landscaping, potholed parking lots, dirty bathrooms, slow or no response to crises, untrained leaders, limited vision, low morale, and the list goes on.

Recently the president of a major passenger airline was heard to say that he makes sure the ashtrays and bathrooms are clean because if they don't care for those details, people will wonder if they care for and service the engines the same way. Total Quality Ministry affects everything—absolutely everything the church does.

Statistics indicate that nearly 30 percent of all Christian churches are near collapse and 40 percent more are sharply in decline. Unhealthy churches cannot carry out healthy ministry. It is time for transformation. Total Quality Ministry can be a vehicle for this transformation. Even many of our Christian colleges and seminaries are floundering. Bold, daring steps need to be taken today!

Major businesses around the world are way ahead of the church when it comes to quality management. Why? Why shouldn't the Christian church be the leader in establishing the guidelines and quality standards? The Christian church used to lead the way in shaping morals, values, ethics, and ideals. Now we aren't even invited into the room. A very influential politician commented that whenever she was invited to an important event in Washington, D.C., she was given strict instructions to never discuss her love for God. If she did, she would never be invited back.

The press has not only an indifferent bias toward Christianity, it often becomes hostile. A major television news personality said that the majority of the people in his business were not only nonchurched, they were anti-church. Our world needs women and men who are committed to Total Quality Ministry and all that goes along with it:

- quality relationships
- quality measurements
- quality processes
- quality values
- quality morals
- quality ethics
- quality leadership
- quality workplaces
- quality programs
- quality care-giving
- quality financial management
- quality strategies
- quality methods

It's Time to Say "Good-bye" to Just Getting By

To paraphrase James Russell Lowell:

Life is a leaf of white paper
Whereon each one of us may write
A word or two—then comes right.

Greatly begin! Now when we have time
But for a line, be that sublime
Not failure, but low aim, is crime.

In ministry, as was stated in the introduction, *good enough is never good enough*. Ministry deserves quality efforts, quality thinking, quality service, and quality management. Many will quickly challenge this and say that by emphasizing quality we are endorsing "works righteousness" or a "theology of glory." Don't be deceived. Quality isn't selling out to triumphalism or trying to out-God God. Quality is placing all that we have and all that we are under God's management. It is about being good stewards. That is where true total quality begins.

Authentic quality begins and ends with God. The more of ourselves—our time, our treasures, our talents, our relationships, and our future—we give to God, the more Total Quality Ministry transpires. As the miracle and magnificence of quality unfolds, we will experience:

Quick Responsiveness to Needs developing
Unity of Purpose growing
Anticipation and Expectation emerging
Leadership Development excelling
Investigating Results improving
Training, Education, and Development increasing
Yields multiplying

Every Christian denomination, education center, mission center, and congregation in the world is one of God's treasures. Total Quality Ministry will certainly be a significant part of ensuring that God's treasure will be strong and healthy into the twenty-first century and beyond.

The Japanese have a word for continuous total quality improvement, *kaizen*. Kaizen is about the commitment to make small improvements in processes every day. Every day the challenge is to find some way to improve even one tenth of one percent in what is done. Continuous improvement is not optional—it is essential.

Inch by Inch, Quality Is a Cinch

This powerful quality attitude and commitment to continuous improvement has transformed the perception of Japanese products from 1960 to today.

1960	Today
Junk	High Quality
Crummy	State of the Art
Second Rate	First Rate
Worst Choice	Best Choice

What changed? Part of the difference is everyone was encouraged to be as inventive and innovative as possible in order to do better tomorrow what was being done today.

What is your next step? Look again at leadership development in Chapter 5. Establish your Quality Council and make your plans.

Clearly God is calling the church to follow the lead of Total Quality Ministry where innovation and excellence penetrate every nook and cranny of the ministry. We can all be optimistic about the outcome because God is already in tomorrow arranging the best and maximizing all the possibilities. As we journey into the fantastic future together, let's strive for quality standards. Quality is a *journey* not a destination! Let's enjoy the journey together. Let's give ministry the best "quality shot" we can, and God will certainly bring to completion the great work that's begun!

Let's Start an Epidemic of Quality—Now

If this book has ignited your fire, if you have been captured by the Total Quality vision and are ready for the next step, contact The JOY Company at 21000 N. 75th Ave. Glendale, AZ 85308 for available resources, consultation, workshops, seminars, and other information.

Notes

Chapter 2
1. Laura Billings, "Impresario," *Minnesota Monthly*, October, 1993.
2. J.M. Juran, *Juran on Quality by Design*, The Free Press, a division of Simon & Schuster, 1992, p.8.
3. Peter F. Drucker, *Managing the Nonprofit Organization*, Harper Collins Publishers, 1990, p.112.
4. Ibid., p.108.
5. George Barna, *User Friendly Churches*, Regal Books, 1991
6. George Barna, *What Americans Believe*, Regal Books, 1991, p.64, 68.

Chapter 3
1. Drucker, p. 112

Chapter 4
1. Juran, p.14.
2. Leith Anderson, *Dying for Change*, Bethany House Publishers, 1990, p. 198.
3. Drucker, p.109.
4. Earnst & Young Quality Improvement Consulting Group staff, *Total Quality: An Executive's Guide for the 1990s*, Business One Irwin, 1990, p.51.

Chapter 5
1. Philip B. Crosby, *Completeness, Quality for the 21st Century*, Dutton, 1992, p.7.
2. Michael Hammer & James Champy, *Reengineering the Corporation*, Harper Collins, 1993, p.105.
3. Earnst & Young, p.28.

Chapter 6
1. Juran, p.124.

2. "Church Membership Initiative," study by the Evangelical Lutheran Church in America, Lutheran Church–Missouri Synod, and Wisconsin Evangelical Lutheran Church, sponsored by Aid Association for Lutherans, 1993.

Chapter 7
1. Stephen R. Covey, *Principle-Centered Leadership*, Simon & Schuster, 1992, p.255.
2. Earnst & Young, p.163.
3. Ibid.

Chapter 8
1. Earl D. Radmacher, *You and Your Thoughts*, Tyndale House Publisher, Inc. 1977, p.51.
2. Russell Chandler, *Racing Toward 2001*, Zondervan Publishing House, 1992, p.231.
3. "Church Membership Initiative."
4. Ibid.